WIRED FOR COACHING THE NEUROSCIENCE FIELD GUIDE

Science-Backed Tools to Elevate Your Coaching Practice

SUMAIYA SULTANA

BlueRose ONE .com
Stories Matter
NewDelhi • London

BLUEROSE PUBLISHERS
India | U.K.

BlueRose ONE.com
Stories Matter
NewDelhi • London

For permissions requests or inquiries regarding this publication, please contact:

BLUEROSE PUBLISHERS
www.BlueRoseONE.com
info@bluerosepublishers.com
+91 8882 898 898
+4407342408967

ISBN: 978-93-7310-213-9

Cover design: Yash Singhal
Typesetting: Namrata Saini

First Edition: November 2025

As I reflect on my journey to write this book, I am driven by a deep calling to elevate the coaching profession beyond its current limitations. After two decades of integrating neuroscience, positive psychology, Clinical Hypnotherapy and NLP in my coaching practice, I've witnessed firsthand the transformative power of psychology informed coaching.

My mission in crafting this work stems from a concerning trend: while the coaching industry expands rapidly, many practitioners lack the psychological foundations needed to facilitate deep, lasting change. Through my research and extensive client work, I've identified this critical gap between traditional coaching approaches and the psychological dimensions that truly drive human transformation.

This book represents the culmination of my research, practical experience, and collaboration with thought leaders in psychology and neuroscience. I've distilled complex theories into practical frameworks that coaches can immediately apply to deepen their impact.

Drawing from over 1,000 client sessions and numerous case studies, I present evidence-based methodologies that bridge the inner and outer aspects of personal development. The tools and techniques shared here have been tested and refined through years of practical application.

I wrote this book for coaches who seek to transcend surface-level interventions and create profound, sustainable change in their clients' lives. Whether you're a novice coach or an experienced practitioner, this work will provide you with the psychological foundations and practical tools to elevate your practice.

The Art of Co-Creating: Understanding the Spirit of Coaching

In a small art studio, an artist named Jin stared at a blank canvas. For months, it had stood there untouched. Every time he picked up a brush, doubt crept in. His earlier works hung on the walls, paintings that had once brought him joy but now felt like reminders of a creativity he'd lost.

One evening, another artist named Mei visited his studio. But instead of giving advice about technique or suggesting what to paint, she pulled up a chair and asked, "What do you see when you look at this canvas?"

Jin began to speak about his frustration, but Mei continued to listen. As he talked, she didn't offer solutions. Instead, she asked questions that made him think: "When was the last time you painted without worrying about the result?" "What would you create if no one else would ever see it?"

Each week, they met. Mei never touched a brush. She simply sat with Jin as he rediscovered his own way. Sometimes he would paint, sometimes just talk. When he got stuck, she would ask, "What's stopping you?" or "What else could this become?"

Gradually, Jin began to see that his creative blocks weren't about lacking skill or ideas. They came from layers of expectations he'd built up over the years. With each conversation, another layer fell away.

One day, Jin realized something had changed. The blank canvas no longer felt like a judge, but like an invitation. The paintings that emerged weren't like his old work, nor were they what he'd imagined they "should" be. They were something new something true to who he'd become.

"You never told me what to paint," Jin said to Mei one day.

"No," she smiled. "The answers were already in you. You just needed someone to help you find them."

From then on, when other artists asked Jin about his transformation, he would say: "The greatest gift wasn't being told what to create, but having someone who helped me clear away what was blocking my own vision."

In coaching, like in art, transformation emerges not from being told what to do, but through a journey of discovery. The story of Jin and Mei illustrates the fundamental principles that lie at the heart of coaching principles that separate it from advice-giving, mentoring, or consulting.

When Mei sits with Jin in front of his blank canvas, she demonstrates what we in coaching call "holding space." She doesn't arrive with preconceived solutions or a blueprint for success. Instead, she creates an environment where Jin can safely explore what's blocking his natural creativity and potential.

The blank canvas represents what we often face in life, possibilities that feel overwhelming or paralyzing. Many people come to coaching expecting to be given a ready-made picture to copy, much like Jin might have expected Mei to tell him what or how to paint. Instead, coaching, like Mei's approach, helps people recognize and remove the layers of "shoulds," expectations, and limiting beliefs that prevent them from accessing their own wisdom.

The weekly conversations between Jin and Mei mirror the coaching journey. Through powerful questions rather than direct advice, through presence rather than prescription, transformation begins to occur. This is what we call "co-creating" in coaching a partnership where the coach walks alongside the client, helping them clear away obstacles and rediscover their own path.

Like a masterpiece waiting beneath layers of paint, your authentic self and wisdom already exist within. Coaching creates the space to peel away what conceals your natural capabilities, helping you discover solutions aligned with who you truly are. A coach's power lies not in expertise about your life, but in their ability to help you reconnect with your own inner knowing.

Contents

CHAPTER 1

From Finding Your Big Why to Raising Your Standards as a Coach

Take a moment to pause. Before we delve into the transformative journey of becoming an extraordinary life coach, I want you to reflect on something profound.

Why are you holding this book in your hands right now?

As your guide through this journey, I'll share my experience first. My path to becoming a life coach wasn't a straight line; it was a calling that emerged from the intersection of purpose and impact. I didn't choose life or executive coaching; rather, coaching chose me through a series of profound realizations and transformative experiences that showed me the immense power of human potential.

For years, I witnessed people settling for less than they were capable of achieving. I saw brilliant minds trapped in cycles of self-doubt, visionaries hesitating to take the leap, and leaders struggling to align their actions with their deepest values. Each observation strengthened my conviction that there was something more I could offer something beyond traditional consulting or therapy.

Coaching, for me, transcends the notion of a mere profession or business venture. It's a vocational calling that demands complete alignment with one's core purpose. When people ask me, "Is life and executive coaching your business or your passion?" my response "It's my purpose manifested through business excellence."

Exercise: Your Turn to Reflect

Take out your pen and paper, answer these questions with complete honesty:

1. **What stirred in your heart when you first considered becoming a life or executive coach?**

2. **When you envision yourself five years from now as a coach, what impact do you see yourself having?**
3. **What transformation are you uniquely positioned to facilitate in others' lives?**

This isn't about finding the perfect answers it's about uncovering your truth. Your "**Big Why**" is the compass that will guide your coaching journey, shape your methodology, and ultimately determine the depth of transformation you create in your clients' lives. Let it be both your foundation and your North Star.

The path to becoming a transformational coach requires more than just good intentions or personal triumph stories. While your lived experience adds invaluable depth to your practice, professional coaching demands a comprehensive understanding of human behaviors, psychological frameworks, and evidence-based methodologies.

Let's explore the different archetypes of coaches I've observed in my years of mentoring coaches:

The Experiential Coach: You've overcome significant challenges and feel called to guide others through similar transformations. Your personal journey provides authentic insights, but remember your experience is one data point in the vast spectrum of human experience.

The Transitional Coach: Perhaps you're pivoting from a corporate career or entering coaching post-retirement, bringing valuable leadership and life wisdom. Your professional experience is an asset, but coaching requires a distinct skill set beyond management or mentoring.

The Therapeutic Coach: Your background might be in counselling or psychology, giving you deep insights into human behaviors. While this foundation is valuable, coaching focuses on future oriented growth rather than past healing.

The Strategic Coach: You excel at systems and solutions, approaching coaching from a pragmatic perspective. Your analytical skills serve you well, but remember that transformation often requires emotional intelligence alongside strategic thinking.

The Transformational Coach: You are driven by a deep desire to catalyze profound change in individuals and organizations. Your strength lies in inspiring breakthroughs, helping clients shift limiting beliefs, and fostering personal evolution. While your visionary approach is powerful, remember that true transformation requires not just insight but also sustainable action and integration

Use a table format Discover Your Coaching Archetype: A Simple Quiz to Reveal Your Natural Coaching Style

Read each statement carefully. Score each one: 2 = Yes / that's totally me! / 1 = Sometimes 0 = Not really me

Questions	Score
1.When someone shares a challenge, I instinctively connect it to lessons from my own life journey. This helps me understand their situation better and offer relevant guidance.	
2. I find myself drawn to frameworks, data, and systematic approaches to problem-solving. I believe the best solutions come from structured analysis and clear action plans.	
3. Understanding the psychological roots of behaviors fascinates me more than quick fixes. I'm naturally curious about why people think and act the way they do.	
4. I excel at seeing business opportunities and helping others optimize their professional potential. My corporate experience gives me unique insights into career development.	
5. I often notice emotional undercurrents in conversations that others might miss. People tell me I have a gift for understanding their unspoken feelings.	
6.Breaking down complex situations into actionable steps comes naturally to me. I enjoy creating clear, measurable paths to achievement.	
7.My own transformation story is what drives me to help others change their lives. I believe personal experience is the best teacher.	

8. I'm energized by exploring innovative solutions and thinking outside conventional boundaries. I enjoy challenging traditional approaches to personal development.	
9. Building long-term relationships and watching gradual progress excites me more than quick wins. I'm patient with the process of deep personal growth.	
10. I naturally focus on future possibilities rather than dwelling on past experiences, allowing me to maintain optimism and help others see potential pathways forward.	

Add your points for:

- Questions 1 + 7 = Your Experiential Score
- Questions 2 + 6 = Your Strategic Score
- Questions 3 + 5 = Your Therapeutic Score
- Questions 4 + 8 = Your Transitional Score
- Questions 9 + 10 = Your Transformational Score

Your Results:

- Highest score = Your Primary Style
- Second highest = Your Secondary Style

My Coaching Journey

I never intended to become a coach. My career began in Learning & Development, where I steadily advanced into roles as a manager, director, and management consultant. Along the way, I naturally embodied my core strengths: Arranger, Connectedness, Empathy, Ideation, and Adaptability. Coaching wasn't something I consciously pursued; it was something I instinctively did. I found immense fulfilment when people shared how our conversations left them feeling empowered, capable, and ready to take on new challenges.

That realization ignited a deeper calling. I immersed myself in formal coaching certifications: Life and Executive Coaching, Hypnotherapy,

Cognitive Behavioral Therapy (CBT), Master Neuro-Linguistic Programming Master Practitioner, Positive Psychology, and Expressive Arts for integral embodiment. Beyond refining my expertise, I began designing coaching certification programs aligned with international standards, shaping the next generation of coaches.

Then came a moment of introspection that deepened my understanding of my journey. During one of my mentoring sessions, a mentee asked, *"What's your success rate in coaching?"* Without hesitation, I responded 100%. Not as a boast, but as a reflection of the profound transformations I had witnessed. Coaching, to me, is not about offering quick fixes or surface level motivation. It is about facilitating deep, sustainable change, helping individuals heal past wounds, break free from limiting beliefs, and cultivate a renewed perspective on life. Over the past 17 years, I have worked with more than 7,000 individuals, using an integrative approach that merges neuroscience, behavioral psychology, and cognitive transformation methodologies.

This book is a culmination of that journey. It is designed to equip you with the essential tools, frameworks, and insights to refine your coaching expertise. Whether you are just beginning or looking to elevate your practice, my goal is to help you become a transformational coach, one who doesn't just inspire change but embodies it.

CHAPTER 2

The Science of Coaching & Behavior Change

What does coaching mean to you? Is it a structured, goal-oriented process designed to drive measurable results? Or is it a deeper, transformative journey where individuals unlock their full potential and make profound shifts in their lives? Perhaps it's both a bridge that connects where a person is today to where they aspire to be, guided by the science of behavior and change.

Behavior is at the core of who we are. It is shaped by experiences, habits, and underlying thought patterns. Neuroscience tells us that behavior is not static; it is malleable, influenced by neural pathways that can be strengthened, altered, or rewired. Every thought we reinforce, every habit we build, and every belief we challenge plays a role in shaping our actions and outcomes.

It's time to discover what Neuro-Coaching is all about. This transformative approach combines neuroscience, psychology, and coaching to unlock the deepest potential in humans. As a psychotherapist, my aim is not simply to provide you with theories; it is rather to give you the tools and processes to make a real, lasting impact on the people with whom you work. You will learn how to guide your clients beyond surface level insights into neurological shifts that promote sustainable improvement.

The Transtheoretical Model - Stages of Change

To facilitate meaningful transformation, coaches must understand the psychological and neurological principles that drive behavior. Here, we explore The Transtheoretical Model. The Transtheoretical Model (TTM), developed by Prochaska and DiClemente, outlines six stages individuals progress through when adopting new behaviors:

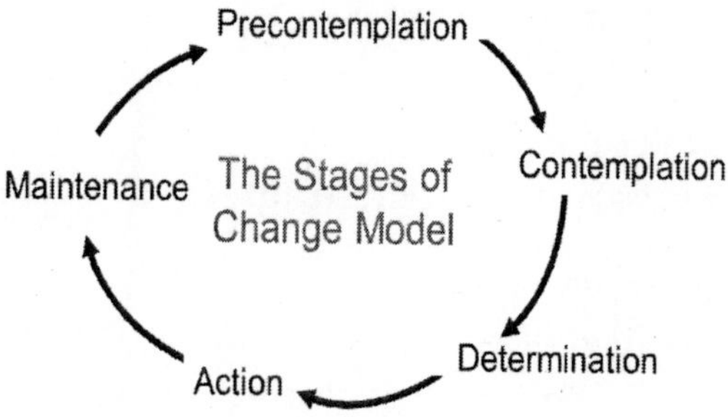

Precontemplation: You may notice your client isn't recognizing there's a problem yet. They'll often say things like "I don't have an issue" or dismiss concerns from others. At this stage, they're not ready to consider change.

Contemplation: Now your client is beginning to recognize the issue. They might say "Maybe there is something to address here..." They see the problem but feel ambivalent about making changes.

Preparation: Your client has decided change is necessary and is getting ready. They're actively seeking information, exploring resources, and making initial plans.

Action: Your client is now implementing changes. They're practicing new behaviors, following through on commitments, and making tangible adjustments to their lifestyle.

Maintenance: Your client has successfully made changes and is focusing on sustaining them. They're developing strategies to prevent relapse and integrating new patterns into their everyday routine.

As a coach, recognizing which stage a client is in allows for tailored interventions that meet them where they are. By aligning your coaching techniques with these stages, you ensure that your interventions are timely, relevant, and effective, fostering lasting behavioral transformation.

Time To Practice

Think of a current or past client struggling with change (e.g., improving work-life balance, building confidence, or adopting a healthier lifestyle).

- Assess Their Stage of Change

- Which stage best describes your client and why?
- What coaching techniques will you apply for this stage?

Coaching vs. Therapy vs. Counselling: Key Differences

As I have observed, coaches sometimes drift into merging coaching, therapy, and counselling, blurring the boundaries between these distinct disciplines. While the intention is to provide comprehensive support, this can lead to ethical concerns, ineffective interventions, and potential harm to clients. Understanding these distinctions is essential for life/executive coaches to maintain ethical practice, ensure client success, and build a strong professional reputation. Although coaching, therapy, and counselling all focus on personal growth and wellbeing, they serve different purposes and follow unique approaches. Recognizing these differences helps individuals choose the right support based on their needs while allowing coaches to practice within their professional scope.

Coaching	**Therapy**	**Counselling**
Future oriented, focuses on personal and professional growth, goal achievement, and maximizing potential.	Explores past and present, supporting emotional wellbeing, healing, and self-awareness.	Addresses present challenges, offering guidance for life transitions, relationships, and decision making.
Encourages self-discovery, clarity, and action toward aspirations.	Facilitates emotional processing, resilience, and deeper self-understanding.	Provides support, coping strategies, and perspective for specific life situations.
Uses goal-setting, accountability, and structured action	Integrates therapeutic models like CBT, psychoanalysis, and	Applies talk therapy, guidance, and solution-focused

Coaching	Therapy	Counselling
plans (e.g., NLP, Positive Psychology).	trauma-informed approaches.	techniques to navigate concerns.
Based on coaching methodologies and structured programs (e.g., ICF certifications).	Rooted in clinical psychology and licensed mental health practices.	Grounded in counseling theories and best practices, tailored to situational needs.
A collaborative, results driven approach with defined milestones.	A reflective, exploratory process with adaptive progress over time.	A supportive, guidance-based engagement for clarity and wellbeing.

Ethical coaching maintains clear boundaries between coaching, counselling and therapy. Coaches help clients achieve future goals while therapists address past traumas. Understanding these distinctions allows coaches to support clients effectively while recognizing when to refer to mental health professionals. The following dos and don'ts will help you navigate these important professional boundaries.

Do's and Don'ts in Coaching

Do's

- **Maintain Professional Boundaries** – Stay within your coaching scope and refer clients to therapists when emotional or mental health issues arise.
- **Use a Goal Oriented Approach** – Focus on helping clients set and achieve actionable goals rather than analyzing past experiences.
- **Practice Active Listening** – Create a safe space for clients to explore their thoughts and insights without judgment.

- **Ask Powerful Questions** – Encourage self-reflection and problem solving rather than offering direct solutions.
- **Follow Ethical Guidelines** – Adhere to coaching standards set by professional bodies like ICF to ensure responsible practice.

Don'ts

- **Don't Diagnose or Treat Mental Health Issues** – Coaching is not therapy; avoid interpreting psychological disorders or offering therapeutic advice.
- **Don't Give Direct Instructions** – Coaching is about guiding, not telling clients what to do. Empower them to make their own decisions.
- **Don't Cross Personal Boundaries** – Keep the relationship professional and avoid over involvement in a client's personal life.
- **Don't Promise Quick Fixes** – Personal growth takes time; avoid guaranteeing instant results.
- **Don't Ignore Confidentiality** – Respect client privacy and only share information with consent or in cases of legal obligation.

By following these do's and don'ts, coaches can maintain ethical integrity, foster trust, and create a positive, goal-oriented coaching experience for their clients.

CHAPTER 2 CONTD

Exploring the Dimensions of Coaching

Coaching today is a multifaceted discipline that extends far beyond performance enhancement or problem solving. It is a deeply human centered practice that helps individuals reconnect with their purpose, realize their potential, and step into meaningful action. As coaching has evolved, so too have its applications spanning industries, roles, and life stages. In this chapter, I offer an overview of key coaching domains that frame much of the work we do as transformational coaches.

While each type of coaching has its own focus, they all share a common foundation: creating space for reflective dialogue, empowering decision making, and honoring the client's inner wisdom. The tools, language, and outcomes may vary, but the heart of coaching remains consistent: it is a partnership designed to bring forth change from within.

Below are some of the most impactful coaching disciplines I've worked with and observed in practice.

1. Leadership Coaching

Leadership coaching focuses on developing the mindset, behaviors, developing competencies and emotional intelligence of individuals in leadership roles. It is not limited to executives; it applies to anyone responsible for influencing others, making decisions, and guiding teams or systems. Through this coaching, leaders reconnect with their **core values**, clarify their **purpose**, and reflect on the **legacy** they want to create.

Common goals in leadership coaching include:

- Enhancing executive presence
- Navigating complex decisions with integrity
- Leading through uncertainty and change
- Developing authentic influence and relational trust

2. Career Transition Coaching

Career transitions, whether self-initiated or forced, can stir a wide range of emotions, from fear to excitement. This form of coaching helps individuals identify **transferrable strengths**, explore new directions, and redefine success on their own terms. It supports clients in aligning career choices with personal meaning, rather than simply chasing roles or titles.

Typical coaching objectives may include:

- Exploring new career pathways or industries
- Reframing setbacks such as layoffs or stagnation
- Building confidence in one's evolving professional identity
- Crafting a narrative that reflects both past success and future aspiration

3. Team Coaching

Team coaching works with groups, not just individuals, to improve collaboration, trust, and shared accountability. Rather than focusing solely on task performance, this approach uncovers **collective strengths**, shared values, and unspoken dynamics that shape the group's identity and culture.

Team coaching often explores:

- Building psychological safety within the team
- Co-creating a shared vision and action plan
- Resolving interpersonal conflict or misalignment
- Celebrating team wins to amplify what works

4. Resilience Coaching

In a world of continuous change, personal and professional resilience is more critical than ever. Resilience coaching helps individuals shift the narrative from **trauma to triumph**, allowing them to reconnect with their inner strength and sense of agency. It is particularly relevant for clients navigating burnout, loss, emotional fatigue, or high-pressure environments.

Key outcomes of resilience coaching include:

- Identifying sources of inner strength and recovery
- Reframing limiting beliefs and emotional narratives
- Cultivating healthy coping strategies and boundaries
- Re-establishing hope and motivation after setbacks

5. Performance Coaching

Performance coaching is results oriented. It supports individuals in achieving specific goals, optimizing their strengths, and improving outcomes in measurable ways. Whether the focus is professional productivity, communication, or mastering new skills, performance coaching helps clients translate insight into action.

Areas commonly addressed include:

- Setting and sustaining high performance habits
- Enhancing time management and focus
- Developing feedback literacy and accountability
- Turning ambition into sustained achievement

6. Life Coaching

Life coaching takes a more holistic approach, encompassing personal fulfillment, life purpose, relationships, and wellbeing. Clients who engage in life coaching are often seeking clarity, alignment, or a deeper connection to their inner compass.

Themes often explored include:

- Life purpose and personal vision
- Creating balance across life domains
- Shifting life patterns that no longer serve
- Making meaningful life transitions

7. Wellness and Mental Fitness Coaching

Distinct from therapy, wellness coaching focuses on proactive self-care, mental clarity, and sustainable lifestyle habits. It integrates elements of mindfulness, mindset shifts, and behavior change. This coaching is especially impactful for professionals dealing with overwhelm, decision fatigue, or chronic stress.

Focus areas might include:

- Establishing mental and emotional hygiene practices
- Managing energy and motivation cycles
- Breaking unhealthy coping mechanisms
- Enhancing presence, calm, and cognitive clarity

8. Coaching for Inclusion and Cultural Intelligence

In today's diverse and interconnected workplaces, coaching that emphasizes **inclusion, belonging,** and **cultural sensitivity** is essential. This domain of coaching helps individuals and leaders recognize their unconscious biases, navigate cross-cultural dynamics, and lead with equity.

Key objectives include:

- Developing inclusive leadership practices
- Enhancing emotional and cultural intelligence
- Addressing bias and microaggressions
- Fostering empathy and allyship in teams

While these categories provide helpful distinctions, it's important to remember that real coaching is **fluid and contextual**. One session may span leadership, wellness, and resilience themes simultaneously. What matters most is the **client's need** in the moment and the coach's ability to meet them there with presence, skill, and intention.

As you explore the methods and tools in the coming chapters, I invite you to remain open. Appreciative Inquiry, which I discuss in detail next, weaves powerfully through all these coaching forms because no matter the context, it always starts with one question: **"What's already working, and how can we build on it?"**

CHAPTER 3
Understanding the Mind: A Neuroscience Perspective

12 Weeks to Rewire - A Story of Change Through Coaching

"Can 12 weeks really change my life?"

That was the question Aarav asked me, sitting across from me during our first coaching session. He looked lethargic, his shoulders slightly slouched, eyes dimmed with a heaviness that didn't need words to explain. "I've been through a lot," he said after a long pause. "The last few years have completely changed me. Trauma, disappointment, a string of failures. I don't think I'm the same person anymore."

I didn't interrupt. This wasn't the time for strategies or frameworks. It was the time to hold space.

He continued, "I'm not sure what I believe in anymore. My habits have collapsed. I wake up tired, feel anxious all day, and I've lost sight of what I used to be passionate about. Honestly, I don't know how coaching can fix all this in 12 weeks."

I nodded gently and replied, "Aarav, we're not here to *fix* you. We're here to help you remember who you are and rewire how you relate to the world now. And for that, your brain is actually your biggest ally."

That was the beginning of our journey a journey that, backed by neuroscience, unfolded week by week into real, visible transformation.

When people think of personal change, they often associate it with slow progress, resistance, and inconsistency. However, neuroscience offers a more empowering perspective. The human brain is inherently adaptable capable of reshaping itself in response to intentional experiences, a phenomenon known as *Neuroplasticity*.

This capacity for rewiring is the very foundation of effective coaching. When guided by neuroscience informed methods, coaching can generate measurable changes in thought patterns, emotional regulation, decision making, and behavior within just a few weeks. Far from being a vague or unpredictable process, transformation becomes a structured and attainable outcome when it works in alignment with the brain's natural systems.

In this chapter, we will explore how consistent coaching grounded in evidence-based neuroscience can facilitate meaningful personal and professional growth within few weeks.

Rewiring Through Neuroplasticity

At the heart of coaching lies the brain's capacity for neuroplasticity the ability to form new neural connections. Each coaching conversation, reflective question, and action step gives the brain an opportunity to learn and rewire. Clients begin replacing limiting beliefs with more empowering ones, shifting from unconscious autopilot behaviors to conscious choices. With repeated reinforcement over weeks, these new pathways become stronger, helping individuals experience lasting change in how they think, feel, and act.

Cognitive Reappraisal: Changing the Inner Narrative: A significant part of coaching involves helping clients *reframe* their perceptions and narratives. This process, known in neuroscience as cognitive reappraisal, activates the prefrontal cortex, the brain's center for logic, planning, and self-control. Clients begin to reinterpret setbacks, not as signs of failure but as data for growth. This reappraisal reduces the overactivity of the amygdala, which is responsible for fear and emotional reactivity, helping the individual develop emotional resilience and clarity.

The Dopamine Loop: Motivation Through Micro-Wins: When clients set meaningful goals and achieve even the smallest wins, the brain releases dopamine a neurotransmitter associated with motivation, pleasure, and reward. Coaching leverages this by breaking goals into manageable steps and celebrating progress. These dopamine "hits" reinforce motivation, making the client more likely to stick with new behaviors. Over the course of 6 to 8 weeks, these micro-wins can build strong momentum and help shift someone from a state of inertia into one of proactive achievement.

Mindfulness and Metacognition: Training the Observer Mind: Another powerful effect of coaching is the cultivation of self-awareness and mindfulness skills rooted in the brain's default mode network and anterior cingulate cortex. Clients learn to *observe* their own thoughts, triggers, and behaviors without judgment. This meta-cognitive skill allows them to respond rather than react, develop emotional intelligence, and gain greater control over their choices. With practice, they begin to notice their internal landscape shifting toward calm presence and intentional action.

Rewriting Habit Loops: Many of our behaviors are driven by deeply wired habit loops in the basal ganglia. Coaching works to interrupt these automatic patterns by helping clients identify triggers, redefine routines, and install new habits that serve their goals. Strategies like habit-stacking, visualization, and anchoring are commonly used to initiate and reinforce new behaviors. With weekly coaching and daily practice, these new routines can take root within a couple of months, replacing long-standing, unproductive habits.

The Power of Reflection and Integration: Every coaching session provides a reflection loop, offering clients space to process, learn, and integrate insights. Reflection activates memory consolidation processes and strengthens the executive functions of the brain, enabling the client to take abstract insight and convert it into practical application. As the weeks progress, clients start to connect the dots between their thoughts, emotions, and outcomes, creating a sense of coherence and confidence in their personal growth journey.

In 10 to 12 weeks, neuroscience-backed coaching can create visible and felt shifts in a person's mindset, motivation, and behavior. Through consistent, intentional work, clients rewire their neural pathways, regulate emotional responses, and install empowering habits. They become more self-aware, more confident, and more resilient. The brain, when coached with care and understanding, becomes the ultimate ally in personal transformation. By aligning with how the brain naturally learns and grows, coaching doesn't just create change it makes that change sustainable.

CHAPTER 4
From Pause to Practice - Coaching Meets Neuroscience

Before diving into this chapter, I took a conscious pause.

After completing the first two chapters, I didn't move forward immediately. Instead, I gave myself time to step back mentally and physically. I travelled to a quiet hill station, not for inspiration, but for clarity. In the absence of meetings, screens, and deadlines, I found space to reflect on where this journey was heading.

During that pause, I revisited my coaching journal, a simple notebook where I had documented session outcomes, client breakthroughs, recurring themes, and reflections. Reading through it, a clear pattern emerged: transformation wasn't driven by conversation alone. The real shifts occurred when insight met application, when the brain started to rewire itself around new habits, beliefs, and emotional responses.

This chapter marks a pivotal shift in the book.

We now move from exploring coaching concepts to understanding how they work beneath the surface at a neurological and behavioral level. The tone from here becomes more grounded, realistic, and implementation-driven. We begin to integrate the science behind sustainable change, focusing on how coaching can be enhanced through the lens of neuroscience.

What do I have for you:

- What happens in the brain during a coaching conversation
- How the nervous system influences growth, motivation, and emotional regulation
- Why some coaching goals stick while others fade
- And most importantly, how to design interventions that align with how the brain learns and adapts

This is where the practice of coaching becomes not only intentional but also informed by neuroscience, behavior, and evidence. Whether you're a coach, a manager, a leader or someone working on your own growth, the chapters ahead will help you move from awareness to action, from insight to sustainable change.

Let's begin this next phase focused, grounded, and ready to make coaching truly transformational.

CHAPTER 5

Coaching the Mind, Language, and Strengths A Triad for Transformation

"The most powerful coaching doesn't push it aligns with the brain's natural rhythm, speaks the client's internal language, and awakens what is already strong within them."

Every experienced coach reaches a point where surface-level techniques are no longer enough. The client is aware, reflective, and even action-oriented yet something still resists change.

At that point, what the coach needs is not more *tools,* but a deeper understanding: how the brain resists and rewires, how language reflects internal models, and how strengths are both map and fuel for transformation. This chapter connects these three levers: neuroscience, neuro-linguistic insight, and positive psychology into a cohesive approach for facilitating change from the inside out.

Lever 1

The Neurobiology of Transformation - Why Safety Comes Before Change

"The brain that got you here won't get you there... but it'll fight like hell to keep you right where you are."

Imagine this you're sitting with your client. They're lit up with excitement, talking about starting that new business, finally speaking their truth, or breaking free from habits that have held them back for years.

Their thinking brain, the prefrontal cortex, is totally on board. It's saying, "Let's do this!"

But fast forward three weeks... they're stuck again. Frustrated and disappointed. Wondering, why they keep hitting the same wall, even though they want to change.

Here's the thing: Most people (and coaches!) think transformation is all about mindset. But real change? It's not just about what you think. It's about what your nervous system feels is safe.

Because when your deeper brain your survival brain feels threatened by change, it pulls the brakes. Not to be difficult, but to protect you.

Change doesn't start with strategy. It starts with safety.

Let's break down what's *really* going on in your client's brain when they're trying to make a big change. We're working with a brain that's been shaped over *millions* of years, and its number one job? Survival. So, when your client decides to quit their job, speak up in a relationship, or try something completely new... the nervous system doesn't go, *"Yay, growth!"*

It goes, *"Uh-oh. Danger."* And here's the catch, it doesn't know the difference between a life-threatening tiger and the emotional risk of launching a new business. To the brain, a threat is a high-risk window.

So, what does it do?

It shuts down the thinking, planning, and dreaming part of the brain (the fancy prefrontal cortex) and hands control back to the primitive parts that say, *"Let's just stay safe and do what we've always done."*

This is why understanding how the brain is wired is a game-changer for us as coaches.

Think of the brain like a three-story building:

- The basement- Reptilian Foundation
- The middle floor - Limbic Layer
- The top floor -Neocortical Aspiration

Each floor has a unique function and in coaching, real transformation happens when we understand how to meet our clients where their nervous system *actually* is, not just where their goals are.

The Reptilian Foundation: The Certainty Seeker

At the foundation of our brain's design lies the brainstem and basal ganglia what neuroscientists refer to as the reptilian brain. This primal system operates with one core rule: familiar equals safe; unfamiliar equals danger. It's not concerned with growth or ambition its sole purpose is survival. So, when a client begins talking about making a change, this part of the brain runs a quick risk assessment. "We've survived this way for decades," it silently insists. "Why mess with what's working?" This isn't conscious resistance or a mindset issue it's the body's ancient intelligence, quietly protecting what it knows.

Coaches often witness this as what we call the body's veto power: a sudden sense of exhaustion before action, unexpected headaches before big meetings, or an overwhelming urge to do something other than the very thing that might move them forward. Recognizing this response is crucial in coaching. It's not failure, it's the nervous system's way of preserving safety. And our work begins with helping clients understand and work with this built-in protector, not against it.

The Limbic Layer: The Emotion Detector

This is where things start to get especially relevant for coaches. The limbic system isn't just a feeling center; it holds surprising authority. In fact, it can override rational thought entirely. Neuroscience tells us that emotional processing happens approximately 500 milliseconds before conscious thought kicks in. That means by the time your client has started to logically reflect on a situation, their emotional brain has already made the call: safe or unsafe.

But the limbic brain asks a different set of survival questions than the reptilian brain. While the reptilian brain is focused on familiarity, "Have we done this before?" the limbic brain is scanning for emotional and social safety. Its questions are more relational: "Will I still belong? Will I be loved? Will I be enough?" These aren't surface-level worries; they're hardwired into us as survival needs. For humans, social disconnection can feel as threatening as physical danger.

Take, for example, a client who wants to set firm boundaries with their family. Their neocortex the logical, thinking part of the brain understands exactly why this is necessary. But their limbic system is firing warnings: "If we let them down, we'll be rejected. And if we're rejected, we're not safe." It doesn't matter that it's the modern world and personal growth is valued. The emotional brain is still running an ancient operating system where rejection = danger, and belonging = survival.

In coaching, this is where deep empathy and emotional safety become essential. Because until the limbic system feels safe, the neocortex won't have a chance to lead.

The Neocortical Aspiration: The Meaning Maker

At the top of our brain's architecture sits the **neocortex** the newest and most complex layer of the brain. This is the part responsible for imagination, reasoning, language, meaning-making, and our sense of purpose. Within this larger structure lies the **prefrontal cortex**, a kind of "executive office" of the brain that handles decision-making, planning, impulse control, and perspective-taking.

While the **neocortex** allows us to dream, reflect, and create, it's the **prefrontal cortex** that helps turn those ideas into action. This is the part most active during coaching conversations when clients set goals, reflect on their behavior, and commit to change. It's the voice inside that says, *"This might be uncomfortable now, but I know it's worth it."*

But here's the key: the neocortex, and especially the prefrontal cortex, can only function at its best when the more primitive brain systems feel safe. If the **reptilian** or **limbic** layers sense danger, even if that danger is emotional or social rather than physical, they hijack the system. Blood flow to the prefrontal cortex is reduced, and stress chemicals like cortisol are

Now that you understand how the **reptilian**, **limbic**, and **neocortical** systems influence change, the **SAFE Framework** gives you a practical, brain-aware coaching tool. It helps you work *with* the nervous system- not against it- so real, lasting transformation can take root.

The SAFE Framework: Practical Neuroscience for Coaches

Real coaching happens at the nervous system level. Here's your practical tool.

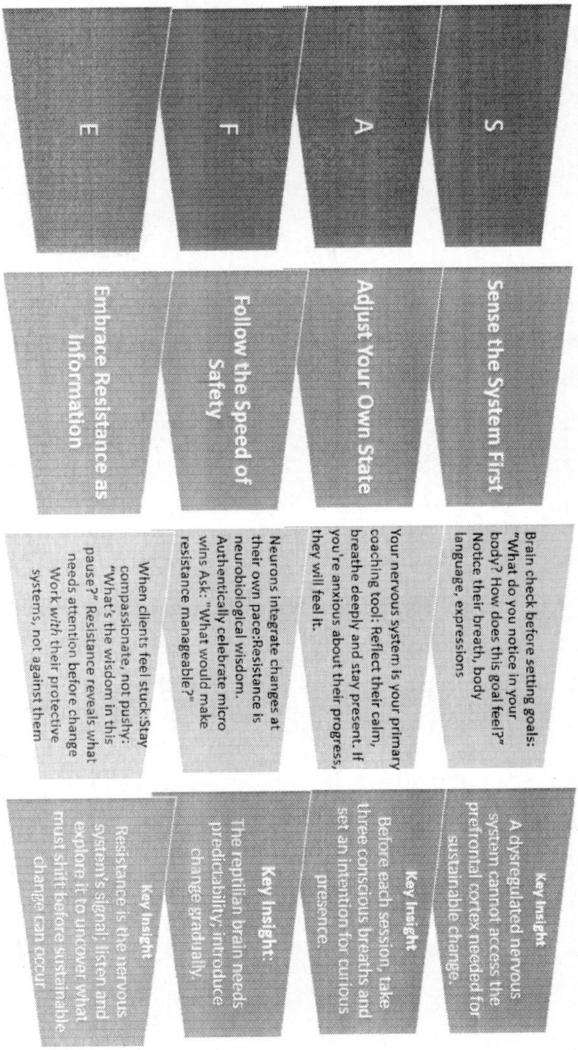

Lever 2: Language as a Lever for Internal Shifts

If the nervous system forms the foundation of transformation, then language is the lever that reshapes perception, belief, and behavior. The **lexicon** a client uses to describe themselves and their situation offers vital clues about which part of the brain is leading the conversation. Are they stuck in survival talk ("I have no choice," "I always mess this up"), or speaking from possibility ("I'm exploring new ways," "This is important to me")? As coaches, our role is to listen for these linguistic cues and gently introduce new language that shifts the internal narrative.

Because language doesn't just describe reality, it constructs it. With consistent use, empowering phrases begin to rewire belief systems, calm the emotional brain, and engage the prefrontal cortex, the part of the brain that makes reflection and action possible. By helping clients speak to themselves differently, we don't just change their words; we open the door to new thoughts, new behaviors, and ultimately, real progress.

Example: A client says, "I know I should speak up in meetings, but I always freeze."

Rather than pushing for action, a coach might respond with, "What would it feel like to say, 'I'm learning to find my voice' instead?"

This small linguistic shift signals safety to the nervous system and opens the door to identity expansion from fear-based avoidance to empowered experimentation.

Lever 3: Neural Pathway

Neural pathways are the brain's dynamic highways, networks of connections that shape how we think, feel, and act. Every experience, thought, or behavior we repeat strengthens these pathways, making certain patterns more automatic and accessible. In coaching, this means that by intentionally focusing on positive thoughts and actions, clients can literally rewire their brains to support resilience, motivation, and well-being.

When a coach helps a client build and reinforce positive neural pathways, it's more than just a technique it's a way to activate circuits tied to capability, identity, and motivation. These neural pathways represent the brain's natural highways that grow stronger with repeated focus on positive thoughts, emotions, and behaviors.

Here's the fascinating part: engaging these neural pathways lights up the brain's dopaminergic system. Clients don't just feel good because they're told they're doing well, but because they're experiencing genuine alignment with their natural capacities and values. Pathways associated with perseverance, curiosity, and self-regulation become well-worn grooves of resilience when consciously practiced. These grooves make it easier for clients to bounce back from challenges and maintain a positive mindset.

At the same time, when clients face emotional lows or resistance, they need more than just quick fixes they need psychological capital. This includes deep reserves of hope, self-efficacy, resilience, and optimism. A skilled coach can sense which of these resources need strengthening and craft thoughtful questions and experiences that restore and build them.

All of this ties beautifully into the idea of neural pathways the brain's highways that grow stronger with repeated use. By focusing on positive thoughts, celebrating small wins, and nurturing empowering behaviors, clients are literally rewiring their brains. This neuroplasticity supports sustained motivation, confidence, and a sense of meaning.

CHAPTER 6

The Ghost Echoes in Mind - Why Your Brain Sabotages Your Best Intentions

Maya stared at her laptop screen, the cursor blinking mockingly in the empty email draft. For the third time that week, she was trying to write a resignation letter from a job that had been slowly draining her soul for two years. And for the third time, her fingers refused to cooperate.

"I don't get it," she told me during our session, her voice carrying that particular exhaustion that comes from fighting yourself. "I know exactly what I want to do. I've researched the company, I have the skills, I even know someone on the inside. But every time I try to take action, it's like there's this invisible force field stopping me."

She laughed bitterly. "My friends think I'm crazy. They keep sending me job postings and motivational quotes. 'Just do it!' they say. 'What's the worst that could happen?' As if I haven't asked myself that question a thousand times."

Maya wasn't lazy. She wasn't lacking in ambition or intelligence. She was trapped by something far more insidious, a ghost in her mental machine, a piece of code written in childhood that was still running her adult life, thirty years later.

And here's the thing that most people don't understand about being stuck: the part of you that wants to change and the part of you that's keeping you stuck are both trying to protect you. They're just using different definitions of safety.

Advice Industry Complexity

We live in the golden age of advice. Online gurus promise to transform your life in seven steps. Social media influencers serve up daily doses of wisdom in digestible, shareable chunks. Bookstore shelves groan under the weight of self-help tomes promising everything from career success to inner peace.

And yet, here we are more anxious, more stuck, more overwhelmed than ever.

I call this the " **Advice Industry,** "a massive system that treats human transformation like a software update. Download the new program, install it, reboot, and voilà, new you! Except humans aren't computers, and personal growth isn't a matter of upgrading our operating system.

The dirty secret of the advice industry is that it's built on a fundamental misunderstanding of how human beings actually change. It assumes that knowledge equals transformation, that awareness automatically leads to action, and that if we just had the right strategy, we'd naturally implement it.

But if that were true, every person who ever read self-help books would be highly effective. Every viewer of a motivational talk on productivity would be wildly productive. Every subscriber to a mindfulness app would be Zen master by now.

The inconvenient truth is that lasting change has very little to do with what you know and everything to do with what your nervous system believes is safe.

The Neuroscience of Self-Sabotage

Let me paint you a picture of what was happening in Maya's brain every time she tried to write that resignation letter.

Deep in her limbic system, an ancient alarm was sounding. Her amygdala, the brain's smoke detector, was treating career change like a saber-toothed tiger. Why? Because thirty years earlier, six-year-old Maya had watched her father lose his job and subsequently spiral into depression. Her young brain had made a simple but powerful connection: career instability equals family chaos equals danger.

This wasn't a conscious thought. Maya couldn't access this memory during our early sessions. But her nervous system remembered, and every time she moved toward leaving her secure (if soul-crushing) job, her internal alarm system activated. Her hands would shake. Her mind would go blank. She'd suddenly remember urgent tasks that needed immediate attention.

This is what I call "**The Ghost Echoes in the Mind,**" unconscious programming that runs our lives from the shadows. It's not malicious; it's protective. But it's using outdated threat assessment software that hasn't been updated since childhood.

Traditional coaching and advice-giving operate at the level of the prefrontal cortex the rational, planning, goal-setting part of the brain. But lasting change requires engaging with the limbic system the emotional, survival-oriented part of the brain that actually drives most of our behavior.

This is why Maya didn't need another career transition strategy. She needed to have a conversation with the part of her that was protecting her from perceived danger.

CHAPTER 7

Blueprints for Becoming, Your map from intention to embodiment.

The human brain is a pattern-seeking machine. When faced with the ambiguous territory of personal change, it craves structure, sequence, and steps. Without a clear map, even the most motivated person can become paralyzed by the infinite possibilities of transformation.

But here's where most goal-setting approaches go wrong: they focus on the destination without adequately exploring the starting point. They skip the crucial step of understanding where you actually are, not where you think you should be or wish you were, but where you honestly, courageously are right now.

This is where the **GROW** model becomes invaluable. Not as another goal-setting framework to add to your collection, but as a bridge-building methodology that honors both the complexity of human psychology and the necessity of practical progress. It's about building a bridge between your current reality and your desired future, a bridge sturdy enough to support not just your conscious intentions but also your unconscious fears.

The Problem with Most Goal-Setting

Before we dive into GROW, let's acknowledge why most approaches to goal-setting fail so spectacularly. Walk into any bookstore in January, and you'll be assaulted by planners, journals, and apps promising to finally make this the year you achieve your dreams. Yet by February, 80% of New Year's resolutions have been abandoned.

The problem isn't the lack of motivation or willpower. The problem is that most goal-setting approaches treat humans like simple machines: input the right goal, add some motivation, apply consistent action, and output success. But humans are complex adaptive systems, not mechanical devices.

We have competing desires, conflicting values, and unconscious fears that sabotage our best intentions. We have past experiences that shape our perception of what's possible. We have nervous systems that equate change with danger, regardless of whether that change is objectively positive.

Traditional goal-setting ignores this complexity. It focuses on the destination that you want to achieve without adequately exploring the starting point, who you are right now, including all your gifts, limitations, fears, and unconscious patterns.

This is like trying to use GPS without allowing it to establish your current location. You might know where you want to go, but without understanding where you are, you'll never get clear directions.

The GROW Model: More Than an Acronym

GROW stands for **Goal, Reality, Options, and Way Forward**. On the surface, it seems almost simplistically straightforward. But like an iceberg, most of its power lies beneath the surface, in the subtle art of asking questions that create insight rather than just information.

The genius of GROW isn't in its structure it's in how that structure creates psychological safety for exploration. Each phase serves a specific function in helping the brain process change without triggering its threat-detection systems.

Let me show you how this works in practice.

G - Goal: The Art of Authentic Aspiration

Most people start with surface-level goals: "I want to lose weight," "I want to get promoted," "I want to find a relationship." These aren't wrong, but they're often symptoms of deeper desires that remain unexplored.

The Goal phase of GROW isn't about setting SMART objectives (though those have their place). It's about excavating authentic desire from beneath layers of should's, supposed-to's, and social conditioning. It's about asking not just "What do you want to achieve?" but "Who do you want to become?"

Consider the difference between "I want to speak up more in meetings" and "I want to feel like I belong and that my contributions matter." The first is behavioral; the second is existential. The first creates pressure to perform; the second creates invitation to be authentic. This distinction matters enormously because surface goals often create surface solutions, while deep goals create lasting transformation.

The Questions That Unlock Authentic Goals:

- What do you really want? (And then ask it again, because the first answer is usually what you think you should want)
- If you achieved this goal, what would that make possible in your life?
- What would success look like not just in terms of outcomes, but in terms of how you'd feel about yourself?
- If fear wasn't a factor, what would you dare to want?

R - Reality: The Courage of Clear Seeing

Once you've clarified your deeper goals, you need to explore your current reality without judgment or the immediate rush to fix things. This isn't just about examining external circumstances but exploring the internal landscape that creates those circumstances.

Most people are remarkably skilled at avoiding their actual reality. They focus on what should be happening, what they wish were happening, or what they think others expect to be happening. But transformation requires radical honesty about what is actually happening in your external world, in your internal world, and in the space between intention and action.

The Reality phase explores not just the facts of your situation but the patterns, emotions, and stories that keep those facts in place. It asks: What's really going on here? What are you feeling? What are you telling yourself? What have you tried before, and why didn't it work?

The Reality Exploration Framework:

- What's actually happening? (Not what should be happening or what you wish were happening)
- What are you feeling in your body when this situation arises?
- What stories are you telling yourself about this situation?
- What patterns do you notice? When does this show up, and when doesn't it?
- What have you tried before, and what were the results?

O - Options: Beyond the Obvious Solutions

Most people, when stuck, suffer from what psychologists call "**functional fixedness**" the inability to see new uses for familiar tools or new approaches to familiar problems. They get trapped in either/or thinking: either I'm confident or I'm scared, either I take bold action or I stay safe, either I'm successful or I'm failing.

The Options phase deliberately expands the field of possibilities by exploring the full spectrum of choices, including some that might seem impractical or even absurd. The goal isn't to find the "right" answer but to break free from the narrow corridor of possibilities that keeps you stuck.

This phase works because it engages the brain's creative networks while temporarily suspending judgment. When we give ourselves permission to consider all possibilities even ridiculous ones, we often discover surprisingly elegant solutions that were hiding in plain sight.

The Options Generation Process:

- If you had unlimited resources, what would you do?
- What would someone you admire do in this situation?
- What's the smallest possible step you could take?
- What's the most outrageous solution you can imagine?
- What would you do if you knew you couldn't fail?
- What would you do if failure didn't matter?

W - Way Forward: The Bridge Between Intention and Action

The final phase of GROW is where intentions transform into commitments. But this isn't about creating elaborate action plans or setting arbitrary deadlines. It's about identifying the next right step that feels both challenging and achievable what I call the "sweet spot" of sustainable change.

The Way Forward phase recognizes that transformation happens through a series of small, consistent actions rather than dramatic leaps. It asks: What's the smallest step you could take that would still constitute meaningful progress? When will you take it? What might get in the way, and how will you handle those obstacles?

This phase is crucial because it's where most people abandon their goals. They create beautiful visions and generate creative options, but they fail to build the bridge between intention and action. The Way Forward ensures that insights translate into actual change.

The Way Forward Elements:

- What's your next concrete step?
- When will you take it?
- What obstacles might arise, and how will you handle them?
- How will you know you're making progress?
- Who or what do you need to support you?

The Neuroscience of Structured Exploration

Why does GROW work when so many other approaches fail? The answer lies in how it engages with the brain's natural processing patterns.

When we face complex challenges, our brains can become overwhelmed by the sheer number of variables involved. This creates what researchers call "cognitive load" the mental equivalent of trying to run too many programs on your computer simultaneously. Everything slows down, and eventually, things start to crash.

GROW reduces cognitive load by breaking complex change into manageable chunks. Instead of trying to solve everything at once, it creates a sequence that mirrors how the brain naturally processes information: from broad to specific, from exploration to commitment, from possibility to practicality.

Each phase also engages different neural networks:

- **Goal** activates the prefrontal cortex and reward systems
- **Reality** engages the insula and interoceptive awareness
- **Options** stimulate the default mode network and creative thinking
- **Way Forward** activates the motor cortex and implementation intentions

This isn't just a coaching framework; it's a neurologically optimized approach to change.

The power of GROW lies not in its parts, but in how they work together to create a safe space for change. Use this worksheet to walk through your own GROW process. Take your time, clarity comes in layers.

GROW Model Coaching Worksheet

GOAL: Excavating Authentic Desire

Surface Goal: What do you want to achieve or change?

Deeper Exploration:

1. If you achieved this goal, what would that make possible in your life?

---

2. What would success look like not just in terms of outcomes, but in terms of how you'd feel about yourself?

---

3. If fear wasn't a factor, what would you dare to want?

---

4. Complete this sentence: "What I really want is to become someone who..."

Your Authentic Goal: (Rewrite your goal based on the insights above)

REALITY: The Landscape of Now

Current Situation: Describe what's actually happening (not what should be happening):

Internal Experience:

1. When you think about this situation, what do you notice in your body?
2. What stories are you telling yourself about this situation?
3. What emotions show up most frequently around this challenge?

Pattern Recognition:

1. When does this challenge show up most intensely?
2. When does it not show up? What's different about those times?
3. What have you tried before, and what were the results?

Resources Assessment:

1. What strengths do you have that are relevant to this situation?

2. Who in your life could support you with this?

____

3. What past experiences of success can you draw upon?

____

____

OPTIONS: Expanding the Field of Possibility

Brainstorm Phase: (No editing, just list every option you can think of, including impractical ones)

1. ____________________
2. ____________________
3. ____________________
4. ____________________
5. ____________________
6. ____________________
7. ____________________
8. ____________________

Expansion Questions:

1. If you had unlimited resources, what would you do?

____

2. What would someone you admire do in this situation?

____

3. What's the smallest possible step you could take?

____

4. What's the most creative/unconventional approach you can imagine?

____

5. What would you do if you knew you couldn't fail?

Option Evaluation: Looking at your list above, which options:

- Feel most energizing?

  ____

- Feel most achievable?

  ____

- Address the root cause rather than just symptoms?

  ____

- Honor both your desire for growth and your need for safety?

  _____

WAY FORWARD: From Intention to Action

Chosen Approach: Based on your exploration above, what approach feels most compelling?

Specific Next Steps:

1. What's your very next concrete action?

---

2. When will you take this action? (Be specific - day and time)

---

3. What's the step after that?

Obstacle Anticipation:

1. What might get in the way of you taking these steps?

---

2. How will you handle these obstacles when they arise?

---

3. What would you tell a friend who was facing these same obstacles?

Support Systems:

1. Who do you need to talk about this commitment?

---

2. What resources do you need to gather?

---

3. How will you celebrate progress along the way?

Success Indicators:

1. How will you know you're making progress?

---

2. What will be different about how you feel?

---

3. What will others notice about you?

Commitment Statement: Write a clear, specific commitment to yourself:

"I commit to ____ by ____ because ____."

Review Date: When will you review your progress? _______________

CHAPTER 8
Let Me Introduce You to AI (No, Not That One)

When most people hear the term *AI*, they instinctively think of **Artificial Intelligence** machines that learn, algorithms that adapt, and systems that simulate human behavior. Artificial Intelligence is, without doubt, reshaping industries, automating decisions, and transforming the way we work and live.

However, there's another AI less widely known, but equally transformative in its domain. It doesn't exist in microchips or clouds; instead, it thrives in conversations, flourishes in organizations, and catalyzes meaningful human change. This is **Appreciative Inquiry**.

While *Artificial Intelligence* is about teaching machines to think, *Appreciative Inquiry* is about helping humans re-think about themselves, their work, and the possibilities ahead.

Understanding Appreciative Inquiry

Appreciative Inquiry (AI), developed by David Cooperrider and Suresh Srivastva in the 1980s, is a strengths-based approach to personal and organizational development. Rooted in the principles of positive psychology, systems thinking, and social constructionism, AI begins with a powerful premise:

"People and systems grow in the direction of what they most persistently ask questions about."

Unlike conventional problem-solving models that focus on identifying what's wrong and fixing it, Appreciative Inquiry shifts attention to what's already working, what's **life-giving**, and what's **possible**. It encourages individuals and organizations to examine moments of excellence, peak experiences, and their core values in order to generate sustainable and inspiring growth.

The Artist's Eye: A Metaphor for Appreciative Inquiry

To better understand this approach, consider the metaphor of an art studio. Picture walking into a creative space that's cluttered half-finished canvases, paint stains on the floor, broken brushes scattered around. A conventional lens might immediately point out the disarray: what needs to be cleaned, what is broken, what has failed.

Now imagine entering that same room with the eyes of an artist. Instead of the mess, you notice a corner where the natural light perfectly highlights a painting in progress. You are drawn to a sketch filled with potential, to the vibrancy of a single color that evokes emotion. You ask, *"What inspired this piece? What story were you trying to tell?"*

That's the essence of Appreciative Inquiry: **not denying what's imperfect**, but choosing to amplify what's already meaningful and filled with potential.

The 5D Cycle of Appreciative Inquiry

Appreciative Inquiry follows a structured yet generative process known as the **5D Cycle**. This model guides the practitioner and client through a coherent journey of discovery, imagination, design, and action.

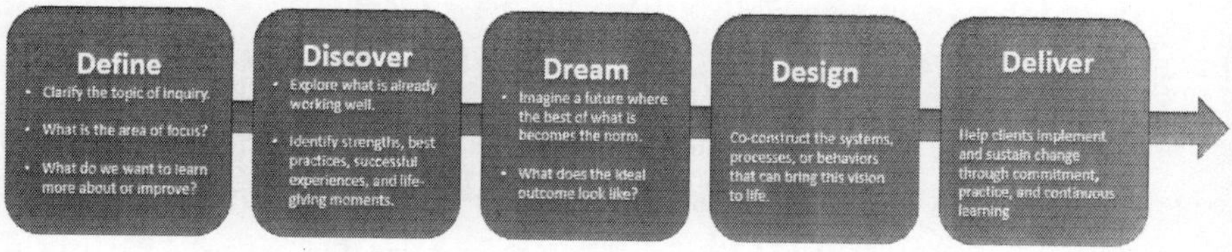

I like the 5D model of Appreciative Inquiry in coaching because it offers a clear yet flexible framework that guides clients from reflection to action in an empowering way. Each stage Define, Discover, Dream, Design, and Destiny, builds on the client's strengths and lived experiences, helping them move beyond problem-solving into possibility-thinking. What I appreciate most is how the model naturally evokes hope, ownership, and creative momentum, allowing clients to envision meaningful goals and take inspired steps with clarity and confidence. It doesn't just create change; it honors and amplifies what's already working well.

Appreciative Inquiry in Coaching: A Personal Reflection

In my coaching practice, I've come to realize that Appreciative Inquiry is far more than a tool it's a mindset that fundamentally shifts the way I engage with clients. It invites both coach and client into a dialogue grounded in strengths, values, and forward movement. Rather than viewing clients as problems to be fixed, Appreciative Inquiry allows me to see them as resourceful individuals with wisdom, resilience, and untapped potential.

I recall working with a client who felt disengaged in their current role and unsure of their next step. In the past, I might have begun the conversation with reflective questions like, *"What's not working for you right now?"* or *"What do you find frustrating about your team?"* While those questions may have surfaced some valuable insights, I noticed they often deepened the client's dissatisfaction or sense of being stuck.

Applying the Appreciative Inquiry approach, I shifted the focus:

"Can you recall a time in this role when you felt most engaged and energized? What were you doing then?"
"What values were being honored in that moment?"
"How might you bring more of that into your present context?"

These questions created a completely different energy in the conversation. The client's posture changed, their voice lifted, and they began to reconnect with their sense of purpose. What I found powerful was how this approach didn't dismiss their current struggle it simply gave them a more constructive foundation to move forward; one built on what already works rather than what's broken.

Appreciative Inquiry has since become a core part of how I coach. It doesn't just create solutions it renews hope, self-belief, and meaningful direction.

How Appreciative Inquiry Enhances Traditional Questioning Techniques

What makes Appreciative Inquiry particularly compelling is not that it replaces other forms of questioning, but that it **enhances and reframes them with a strengths-based lens**. In traditional coaching, questions often arise from a desire to diagnose or dissect. While this can be useful for problem-solving, it also risks placing the client in a defensive or deficit-oriented mindset.

Let's take a closer look at how Appreciative Inquiry interacts with other question types:

- **Open-ended questions** give clients space to express themselves, but without clear focus, they may lead to surface-level responses or venting. When reframed through AI, open-ended questions become more intentional, such as:
  "What past experiences made you feel most alive and fulfilled in your work?"
  This encourages not just openness, but **exploration of strengths** and what matters most.
- **Closed-ended questions** are often used to clarify facts or elicit a yes/no response, such as:
  "Do you feel supported by your manager?"
  In an Appreciative Inquiry framework, a similar question might be transformed into:
  "Can you share a moment when you felt truly supported and seen by your manager?"
  The shift creates a richer, narrative-based response that builds emotional engagement and insight.
- **Reflective questions**, while valuable for self-awareness, can often dwell on pain or limitation if not balanced. For example,
  "Why do you think you failed to meet that goal?"
  might be reframed through AI as:
  "Can you recall a goal you did achieve, and what strengths you

drew upon to reach it?"

Rather than analyzing failure, the focus is on replicating success, which can still lead to learning but without reinforcing self-doubt.

This comparison highlights that Appreciative Inquiry is not just a **technique of questioning**, but a **reorientation of intent**. It prioritizes what energizes the client, what gives them life, and what patterns of success they can build upon. This distinction becomes especially important when coaching clients who are stuck, discouraged, or burned out those who benefit more from being reminded of their capacity than being reminded of their gaps.

Below are **5 different coaching scenarios** with **5 Appreciative Inquiry-inspired questions** for each. These are framed to spark **insight, reflection, and growth** without explaining the basics perfect for an advanced coaching guide or practitioner resource.

Coaching with Appreciative Inquiry: Situational Question Bank

As coaches, we've all seen it that moment when a single, well-timed question shifts everything. The energy changes, the eyes light up, and something clicks. But what actually makes a question *transformational*? It's not just about being clever or deep. It's about asking something that helps the client reconnect with their strengths, their values, their vision. It's about guiding them to what's possible, not just what's wrong.

Here are 5 coaching scenarios, each with 5 Appreciative Inquiry-inspired questions to spark reflection, build momentum, and help clients reconnect with their strengths and purpose.

1. Leadership Coaching

When coaching leaders, the goal is to help them rediscover what kind of leader they truly are at their best and how to lead with authenticity, influence, and intention.

Use these questions to guide that journey:

1. *Tell me about a time when you felt most aligned with your leadership values what was happening?*
2. *What feedback have you received that affirmed the kind of leader you aspire to be?*
3. *What legacy do you hope your team will remember you for?*
4. *When have you led in a way that felt both authentic and impactful?*
5. *If you could amplify one leadership quality you already possess, which one would it be and why?*

2. Career Transition Coaching

Clients in transition often feel stuck between who they were and who they want to become. Your role is to help them connect past wins with future direction.

Ask these to uncover strengths and reframe the path forward:

1. *Can you share a moment in your career when you felt deeply fulfilled what made it so meaningful?*
2. *What skills or qualities have helped you succeed across different roles or industries?*
3. *Who were you at your best in your previous role, and what parts of that self do you want to carry forward?*
4. *What does "success" mean to you now and when have you felt closest to it?*
5. *What parts of your past experience would you love to reimagine in your next career move?*

3. Team Coaching

Team dynamics flourish when we highlight shared wins and appreciate each individual's contribution to the whole.

Use these questions to help teams rediscover what works:

1. *When has the team worked together exceptionally well what contributed to that moment?*
2. *What strengths does each team member bring that make collaboration easier or richer?*
3. *What are you most proud of achieving as a team, and how did you get there?*
4. *When did you feel most connected as a team and how can we recreate that environment?*
5. *If your team operated at its absolute best consistently, what would that look and feel like?*

4. Resilience Coaching

Life throws curveballs. These questions help clients reflect on their capacity to rise, endure, and even thrive through adversity.

Tap into their inner resources with these prompts:

1. *Tell me about a time you bounced back from adversity. What helped you move forward?*
2. *What personal resources or habits supported you during challenging times?*
3. *What stories do you carry of strength and survival that still empower you today?*
4. *Who have you been at your strongest, and how can you access that version of yourself now?*
5. *What mindset shift helped you reframe a tough situation into an opportunity?*

5. High-Potential Coaching

For high-performing individuals, coaching is about stretching existing strengths and creating clarity around their future.

Fuel their growth trajectory with these AI-based questions:

1. *What achievements have surprised even you in the past year, and what made them possible?*
2. *When do you feel most "in flow" while working, what are you doing?*
3. *What feedback or recognition have you received that affirmed your unique potential?*
4. *What would it look like if you stretched your strengths just 10% more?*
5. *If you were to create your ideal growth path, based on what energizes you, what would it include?*

Each of these questions is more than a prompt; they are invitations. Invitations for clients to see themselves clearly, celebrate what works, and build a future grounded in what gives them life.

Part B

From Fixing to Flourishing – A New Way to Coach

Let's be honest, most clients don't come into coaching sessions announcing, "I'm here to discover my full potential!" More often than not, they arrive with a sense that something isn't working. It could be dissatisfaction in their career, strain in their relationships, a recurring internal conflict, or just a lingering feeling of being stuck. As coaches, we're naturally trained to listen for what's not working, to spot patterns, and to help guide clients through their challenges.

And while that's a critical part of the coaching process, it's not the only part. In fact, it might not even be the most transformative part.

This is where **Positive Psychology** offers us a profound shift in perspective. It gently invites us to move away from the default lens of "fixing" and instead explore the deeper terrain of *flourishing*. It encourages us to ask not just, "What's wrong here?" but more importantly, "What's strong here?"

This shift changes everything. When coaching is grounded in Positive Psychology, it stops being a tool for fixing problems and starts becoming a process for unlocking potential. It moves us beyond the role of troubleshooters and into the space of possibility architects. We're no longer just helping people avoid what they fear, we're helping them move toward what truly matters to them.

This doesn't mean we ignore struggle, pain, or discomfort. In fact, we make space for it with compassion and curiosity. But we don't *center* our coaching around the problem. Instead, we anchor it in the client's capacity, their values, strengths, hopes, and past successes. We believe that the solution is not just in what they need to change, but in *who they already are* at their best.

To understand this shift, imagine a client arrives feeling emotionally "flat" disconnected from their role, burnt out, unsure of their next step. A traditional approach might start with an analysis of what's causing the burnout or what external factors need to be addressed. And while that's helpful, it often keeps us stuck in the weeds.

Now, try shifting the question: "Can you tell me about a time when you felt energized in your role? What were you doing then? Who were you being?"

Watch what happens. The client's tone softens. Their posture lifts. Their eyes light up as they recall a memory where they felt capable, creative, and alive. That energy is not trivial it's a breadcrumb trail back to their strengths, values, and deeper purpose. It's a clue to what *gives them life,* and that's what we're here to follow.

In this way, coaching becomes less about correcting the past and more about co-creating the future.

One of the metaphors I often use with clients is this: Imagine your life is a vehicle. When something's off, it's like a flat tire. Sure, we can patch the tire that's needed. But what if, instead of just fixing the flat, we tuned the whole engine, upgraded the fuel, and realigned the direction of the journey? That's the difference between surviving and truly thriving.

This is the promise of Positive Psychology in coaching. It invites us to work from the inside out, to trust that each person has innate strengths, and to coach them from the belief that flourishing is possible regardless of where they begin.

It's also important to remember the difference between therapy and coaching, especially when using Positive Psychology. Therapy often focuses on healing pain, resolving trauma, and addressing dysfunction. It's deeply valuable and needed. Coaching, on the other hand, is future-facing. We don't diagnose or treat; we explore and expand. We ask questions like:

"What makes you come alive?"

"What helps you feel fulfilled and perform at your best?"

"What possibilities are waiting to be lived into?"

We're not rescuing. We're not repairing. We're reconnecting people with their potential and helping them design lives that reflect it.

As you continue your coaching journey, whether in life coaching, executive coaching, or both I encourage you to begin each session not by asking, "What's the problem?" but by exploring, "Where does this client already shine?" Let your coaching conversations become a mirror to their strengths and a map to their future.

Because here's the truth: most people aren't broken. They're just temporarily disconnected from their best selves. And your role, as a coach, is to guide them back home.

In the chapters that follow, you'll see how Positive Psychology can help you facilitate meaningful, lasting change, grounded in evidence and led by the heart.

Let's Begin!

CHAPTER 9

The PERMA Pulse – Coaching That Builds a Flourishing Life

Now that we've explored the shift from fixing to flourishing, it's time to introduce a framework that helps us bring that shift into daily coaching practice. If there's one model from Positive Psychology that I return to again and again in both life and executive coaching, it's the **PERMA model**. Simple, powerful, and deeply human, it gives us a way to understand what well-being really looks like and how to help our clients nurture it. Let me introduce you to a model that has completely transformed how I track, measure, and guide well-being in coaching: **PERMA**.

Developed by Martin Seligman, the founder of Positive Psychology, PERMA is not just a clever acronym. It's a practical and powerful lens through which we can explore what it really means to flourish, whether someone is navigating burnout, making a big career move, or simply trying to live a more meaningful life.

What is PERMA?

PERMA stands for five pillars of well-being:

- **P** – *Positive Emotion*: joy, gratitude, contentment
- **E** – *Engagement*: flow states, deep absorption in meaningful tasks
- **R** – *Relationships*: authentic connection and supportive bonds
- **M** – *Meaning*: a sense of purpose or service beyond the self
- **A** – *Accomplishment*: progress, mastery, and achieving goals

Now here's the magic: you don't have to teach this model as a lecture in your sessions. Instead, you *use* it like a pulse check, a living diagnostic tool to guide reflection and growth.

Here's an instance for you to apply the PERMA model. Ask the client to rate each domain on a scale from **1 (very low)** to **10 (very high)** based on how things are *currently* going in that area.

Start by asking

"On a scale of 1 to 10, how would you rate how things are going for you in the following areas?"

- **P – Positive Emotion:** How often are you experiencing joy, gratitude, or emotional uplift?
- **E – Engagement:** How absorbed or energized do you feel by your daily work and activities?
- **R – Relationships:** How satisfied are you with the quality of your personal and professional relationships?
- **M – Meaning:** How connected do you feel to a deeper purpose or sense of meaning in your life or work?
- **A – Accomplishment:** How proud are you of your recent progress or achievements, big or small?

Your client thinks for a moment and responds:

> Positive Emotion – 4 Engagement – 6 Relationships – 8 Meaning – 3 Accomplishment – 9

At a glance, you can already spot a pattern: This is someone who is *performing well* and *has good connections*, but they're feeling emotionally drained and disconnected from a deeper sense of purpose. They're doing the work but not necessarily feeling it.

What Next?

Use the PERMA Coaching Table to Guide the Conversation

Once you've identified which areas scored low (in this case, **Positive Emotion** and **Meaning**), you can turn directly to the table below. This gives you clear cues on what to listen for, what to ask, and how to support the client moving forward.

PERMA Tool for Coaches – Application Table

PERMA Element	What to Observe	Coaching Prompt	Action You Can Take
P – Positive Emotion	Client's emotional tone, energy, presence of joy, gratitude, humor, or peace	"What made you feel joyful or grateful recently?"	Help client identify and build small, consistent habits that increase joy or calm
E – Engagement	Level of interest, motivation, and absorption in daily tasks or goals	"When did you last lose track of time doing something meaningful?"	Reconnect client with strengths and re-align goals to include more energizing activities
R – Relationships	Quality and depth of personal/professional connections; signs of isolation or support	"Who makes you feel supported, heard, or inspired?"	Explore communication patterns, set boundaries, or encourage intentional connection
M – Meaning	Signs of purpose, value alignment, direction, and contribution	"What are you doing today that truly matters to you?"	Help client define or rediscover values, legacy goals, or meaningful side projects
A – Accomplishment	Sense of progress, confidence, self-worth through achievement	"What have you achieved recently that you feel proud of?"	Celebrate wins, redefine success, set achievable micro-goals and milestones

Here's a sample dialogue of Coach & Client post PERMA

Coach: "You mentioned you're feeling low in joy and not very connected to purpose right now. Let's start with something simple, what's something that brought you joy or peace recently, even for a moment?"

Client: "Honestly? Walking my dog without checking emails felt amazing."

Coach: "That's a beautiful moment of presence. What would it look like to build more of those micro-joys into your day?"

[Client and coach co-create a simple practice around digital-free walks, or blocking time for quiet reflection.]

Coach (later): "And in terms of meaning, what part of your current work or life feels aligned with what really matters to you? Or is there a time in your past when your work felt more purposeful?"

Client: "Two years ago, I worked on a campaign for a cause I believed in. It wasn't the biggest budget, but I felt proud of it."

Coach: "What would it look like to bring that sense of contribution into your current role?"

[This leads to a values conversation and potentially a side project or advocacy initiative.]

Coach's Tip

- The **PERMA Pulse Check** gives you a *diagnosis* and a snapshot of your client's well-being.
- The **PERMA Coaching Table** gives you the *direction* with powerful questions and practical steps.

You can use this process at the **start of an engagement, midway through a long-term coaching relationship**, or when a client **hits a plateau.** Clients often don't realize what's missing until they see it laid out. And once they do, change becomes not only possible but deeply motivating.

CHAPTER 10

Moments That Matter: How Brief Reflections Spark Deep Change

Evokes emotional resonance while reinforcing transformation.

From my journal, after a 7-minute coaching intervention that changed a client's leadership journey.

In my last 12 years of coaching executives and mentoring life coaches, I've discovered that transformation doesn't always require grand gestures or lengthy interventions. Some of the most profound shifts I've witnessed have emerged from what we call **"micro-moments of meaning,"** brief, intentional exercises that can be seamlessly woven into coaching sessions to create lasting positive change.

These micro-moments are like drops of water that eventually carve through stone. They're brief enough to avoid resistance, meaningful enough to create impact, and practical enough to be implemented in real-time during coaching conversations. For coaches working with time-pressed executives or clients who struggle with longer reflective practices, these tools become invaluable.

Understanding Micro-Moments: The Science Behind Small Interventions

Micro-moments of meaning operate on the principle of positive priming, the psychological phenomenon where brief exposure to positive stimuli influences subsequent thoughts, feelings, and behaviors. When we create these intentional pockets of positivity during coaching sessions, we're essentially rewiring neural pathways toward more optimistic and resilient thinking patterns.

The research from positive psychology demonstrates that positive emotions broaden our thought-action repertoires, making us more creative, open, and solution-focused. However, what many coaches don't realize is that these benefits can be activated through interventions as brief as thirty seconds to three minutes.

During a coaching session with Vidya Rastogi, an overwhelmed marketing director, I noticed her shoulders tense whenever we discussed her team dynamics. Instead of diving deeper into the problem, I introduced a micro-moment:

"Hey Vidya! before we continue, I want you to think of one person on your team who made you smile this week." Just hold that image for a moment. Within thirty seconds, her entire demeanor shifted, her shoulders relaxed, and she was able to approach the same challenges from a more resourceful state.

The Neuroscience of Brief Interventions

The brain's neuroplasticity allows for rapid state changes through focused attention. When we guide clients through micro-moments of meaning, we're activating the prefrontal cortex the brain's executive center, while simultaneously engaging the limbic system's positive emotion networks. This dual activation creates what neuroscientists call "positive neuroplasticity," the brain's ability to form new neural pathways around positive experiences.

These brief interventions work because they don't overwhelm the brain's processing capacity. Unlike longer exercises that might trigger resistance or cognitive fatigue, micro-moments slip past our mental defenses and create gentle shifts in perspective.

Core Principles for Creating Micro-Moments

Principle 1: Intensity Over Immediacy

Intensity Micro-moments work best when they're implemented in real-time during coaching conversations. The goal isn't to create dramatic breakthroughs but to introduce subtle shifts that compound over time.

Principle 2: Specificity Creates Stickiness

Vague positive affirmations rarely create lasting change. Effective micro-moments are specific, sensory-rich, and personally meaningful to the client.

Principle 3: Integration, Not Isolation

These exercises should feel like natural extensions of the coaching conversation rather than forced interruptions. They work best when they emerge organically from the client's current state or challenge.

Principle 4: Repetition Builds Resilience

The power of micro-moments lies in their cumulative effect. Regular exposure to brief positive interventions gradually shifts the client's default emotional and cognitive patterns.

Essential Micro-Moment Techniques for Coaches

The 60-Second Strength Spotlight

When clients are stuck in problem-focused thinking, this technique rapidly shifts their attention to their capabilities. "I want you to think of a time in the last month when you handled a difficult situation really well. Take a moment to remember how you felt, what you did, and what strengths you drew upon."

I used this technique with a senior manager who was struggling with imposter syndrome before a major presentation. Within one minute, he reconnected with his confidence and approached the presentation from a place of strength rather than fear.

The Gratitude Micro-Dose

Instead of asking clients to list multiple things they're grateful for, focus on one specific appreciation. "What's one small thing that happened today that you're genuinely grateful for? Tell me about it in detail."

This technique works because specificity activates the brain's reward centers more effectively than generalities. When clients describe their gratitude in detail, they're essentially reliving the positive experience.

The Future Self Check-In

This thirty-second exercise helps clients tap into their intrinsic motivation and values. "Imagine yourself six months from now, having successfully navigated this challenge. What would that version of you want to tell you right now?"

This technique is particularly powerful with executive clients who are caught in short-term thinking patterns. It rapidly expands their perspective and connects them with their deeper purpose.

The Energy Audit

When clients feel depleted or overwhelmed, this micro-moment helps them identify sources of positive energy. "Think about your last week. What was one activity, interaction, or moment that genuinely energized you? What made it different?"

This exercise often reveals insights about what truly matters to the client and helps them make more conscious choices about how they spend their time and energy.

The Strength Transfer

This technique helps clients recognize how their strengths can be applied to current challenges. "You mentioned you're great at building relationships with customers. How might that same skill apply to the challenge you're facing with your team?"

Measuring the Impact of Micro-Moments

One of the most frequent questions I receive from coaches is: "How do I know if these brief interventions are actually working?" The challenge with micro-moments is that their effects can be subtle and cumulative, making them harder to track than traditional coaching outcomes. The key is understanding that micro-moments create both immediate and long-term changes. Despite their brevity, micro-moments create observable changes that can be systematically tracked. Here are the key indicators I've learned to watch for during and after these interventions:

- Immediate shifts in client energy, posture, or tone
- Changes in language patterns (from problem-focused to solution-focused)
- Increased client engagement and participation
- Improved ability to generate options and solutions
- Enhanced emotional regulation during challenging topics

With one client, tracking these micro-interventions revealed that her confidence levels increased by 40% over three months, as measured by her own self-assessments and 360-degree feedback from colleagues.

3 Common Pitfalls of Overusing Micro-Moments and How to Avoid Them

1. The effectiveness of micro-moments depends on their strategic use. Overusing them can make sessions feel artificial or manipulative. Use them judiciously, when they emerge naturally from the coaching conversation.
2. Micro-moments should never be used to bypass legitimate concerns or emotions. They work best when they complement, rather than replace, deeper exploratory work.
3. These exercises are most effective when clients can integrate them into their daily lives. Always help clients identify how they can apply these techniques between sessions.

Creating Your Micro-Moment Toolkit

As a coach, developing your own collection of micro-moment techniques is essential. Start with the exercises outlined in this chapter, but also create variations that match your coaching style and client needs. Consider:

- Your client's communication style (visual, auditory, kinesthetic)
- Their current emotional state

- The session's overall objectives
- Time constraints
- Cultural considerations

To effectively integrate micro-moments into your coaching practice:

1. **Start Small**: Begin with one or two techniques that feel natural to you
2. **Practice Timing**: Learn to recognize optimal moments for these interventions
3. **Develop Sensitivity**: Pay attention to your client's responses and adjust accordingly
4. **Create Rituals:** Consider beginning or ending sessions with brief positive practices

I've come to believe that the best coaching isn't always grand it's timely, present, and precise. Micro-Moments of Meaning make our work more human, agile, and lasting. In the stillness of a pause, the warmth of a remembered win, or the power of a single word, transformation quietly takes root. We don't always need more time, just more intention. Because meaning doesn't always arrive in the hour; often, it hides in the minute.

CHAPTER 11
The Strengths Spotlight

Discovering Signature Strengths with the VIA Framework

Why Strengths-Based Coaching Matters

Drawing from the valuable resources at www.viacharacter.org, I've applied these tools in my own practice and want to share their benefits with fellow coaches. Traditional coaching typically starts with identifying problems, "What needs fixing? "But what if we flipped the script to ask, "What's already working well?" This fundamental reframe is the cornerstone of strengths-based coaching, a positive psychology methodology that empowers clients to build upon their existing assets rather than dwelling on their deficits.

When we examine the brain's response to strengths-based feedback, we observe activation in the ventromedial prefrontal cortex, the region associated with self-referential processing and positive self-regard. This neurological response explains why clients often experience immediate shifts in posture, energy, and cognitive flexibility when they recognize their authentic strengths.

The VIA Framework: A Scientific Foundation

The VIA Classification of Character Strengths developed by psychologists Christopher Peterson and Martin Seligman is the most researched, practical, and accessible framework for identifying inner capacities that contribute to a meaningful life. Unlike skill-based inventories, the VIA focuses on core character traits, those morally valued parts of us that influence our thoughts, emotions, and behaviors.

VIA stands for Values in Action. The framework offers a classification of 24 universal character strengths, clustered under 6 core virtues:

Virtue	Character Strengths
Wisdom	Creativity, Curiosity, Judgment, Love of Learning, Perspective
Courage	Bravery, Perseverance, Honesty, Zest
Humanity	Love, Kindness, Social Intelligence
Justice	Teamwork, Fairness, Leadership
Temperance	Forgiveness, Humility, Prudence, Self-Regulation
Transcendence	Appreciation of Beauty, Gratitude, Hope, Humor, Spirituality

These strengths are considered trait-like, meaning they are relatively stable but can also be developed. Research shows that when individuals use their top 5 signature strengths regularly, they experience higher levels of subjective well-being, resilience, job engagement, and goal attainment.

The Neuroscience of Strengths Recognition

Research in positive psychology reveals that strengths utilization triggers dopamine release, the neurotransmitter associated with reward and motivation. This explains why clients who regularly engage their signature strengths report higher levels of intrinsic motivation and sustained engagement. The key lies in helping clients recognize these dopamine moments during coaching conversations. Different character strengths activate distinct neural networks. Curiosity engages the anterior cingulate cortex and the brain's novelty-seeking systems. Perseverance activates the prefrontal cortex's executive control networks. Kindness stimulates the oxytocin system and mirror neuron networks associated with empathy.

Understanding these neurobiological foundations helps coaches recognize when clients are operating from their strengths versus when they're forcing behaviors that don't align with their natural wiring.

Clients often report feeling "effortless" when using their signature strengths. This reflects the brain's efficient processing when working within its preferred patterns.

The Four Phases of Strengths-Based Coaching

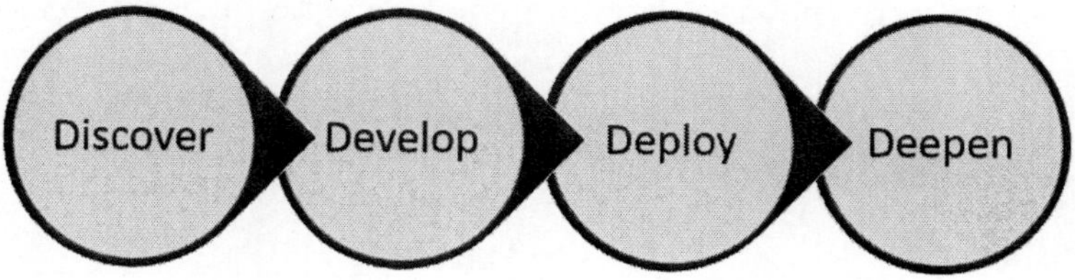

Strengths-based coaching unfolds through four dynamic phases that transform how clients see and use their natural gifts:

Phase 1: Discover

What makes you come alive? This phase uses assessments and reflective conversations to uncover your unique strengths and talents. Coaches help clients identify their natural talents and understand the meaning of strengths from their perspective. It's about recognizing patterns of excellence already present in your life.

Phase 2: Develop

Now we go deeper. Clients learn to understand their strengths more fully, how they show up in different situations, and what conditions help them flourish. This is where raw talent begins to transform into refined capability.

Phase 3: Deploy

Time to put strengths to work! Clients strategically apply their strengths to real challenges and goals. This phase is about intentional action using what you do best to create the outcomes you want.

Phase 4: Deepen

The final phase embeds strengths into daily life. Clients build systems and environments that support ongoing strength development, creating sustainable change that lasts beyond the coaching relationship.

This framework moves clients from "fixing what's wrong" to "amplifying what's right" a journey that feels more natural, energizing, and ultimately more effective.

Implementation Worksheet

Client Name: ________________ **Date:** ________________ **Session:** ________________

Phase 1: DISCOVER

"What makes you come alive?"

Strengths Identification

- **Complete VIA Character Strengths Survey from the website (www.viacharacter.org)**

Reflection Questions

1. **Peak Performance Moments: Describe 3 times when you felt most successful and energized:**
   - **Situation 1:** ________________________________
   - **Situation 2:** ________________________________
   - **Situation 3:** ________________________________
2. **Natural Talents: What do people consistently compliment you on?**

---

3. **Energy Givers: What activities make you lose track of time?**

Top 5 Identified Strengths

1. ______
2. ______
3. ______
4. ______
5. ______

Phase 2: DEVELOP

"Going deeper into your strengths"

Strengths Deep Dive

For each of your top 3 strengths, complete:

Strength 1: ______

- **How does this show up in your work?** ______
- **How does this show up in relationships?** ______
- **What conditions help this strength flourish?** ______
- **When might this strength become a weakness?** ______

Strength 2: ______

- **How does this show up in your work?** ______
- **How does this show up in relationships?** ______

- **What conditions help this strength flourish?**

  ____

- **When might this strength become a weakness?**

  ____

Strength 3: ______________________________

- **How does this show up in your work?**

  ____

- **How does this show up in relationships?**

  ____

- **What conditions help this strength flourish?**

  ____

- **When might this strength become a weakness?**

  ____

Development Planning

Skills to build around your strengths:

- **Strength 1:**

  ____

- **Strength 2:**

  ____

- **Strength 3:**

  ____

Phase 3: DEPLOY

"Put strengths to work"

Current Goals & Challenges

List 3 current goals or challenges:

1. ______________________________
2. ______________________________

3. ______________________________

Strengths Application Strategy

For each goal/challenge, identify which strengths to use and how:

Goal 1: ____________________

- **Primary strength to use:**
  ____
- **Specific action steps:**
  ____
- **Success metrics:**
  ____

Goal 2: ____________________

- **Primary strength to use:**
  ____
- **Specific action steps:**
  ____
- **Success metrics:**
  ____

Goal 3: ____________________

- **Primary strength to use:**
  ____
- **Specific action steps:**
  ____
- **Success metrics:**
  ____

Weekly Action Plan

This week I will:

- ______________________________
- ______________________________

- ____

Phase 4: DEEPEN

"Embedding strengths into daily life"

Environmental Design

How can you structure your environment to support your strengths?

- **Physical workspace:** ________________________________
- **Daily routines:** ________________________________
- **Relationships:** ________________________________

Strengths Partnerships

Who can complement your strengths?

- **Areas where you need support:** ________________________
- **People who have complementary strengths:** ______________
- **How to build these partnerships:** ______________________

Sustainable Systems

What systems will help you maintain focus on strengths?

- **Daily practices:** ________________________________
- **Weekly reviews:** ________________________________

- **Monthly assessments:** ______________________

Long-term Vision

In 6 months, how will you be using your strengths differently?

____

____

____

Coach Notes & Observations

Session insights:

____

____

Client breakthroughs:

____

____

Areas for continued focus:

____

____

Next session priorities:

____

____

____

Client Reflection

What was most valuable about this session?

____

What will you commit to before our next meeting?

____

What support do you need from me as your coach?

___

___

Note: Strengths-based coaching is about amplifying what's already working. Focus on building from a place of natural talent and authentic energy.

CHAPTER 12
The SOAR Model

While most coaching models start by identifying problems to fix or gaps to close, the SOAR model takes a radically different approach. It begins with a simple yet powerful premise: transformation happens most effectively when we build on what's already working. SOAR an acronym for **Strengths, Opportunities, Aspirations, and Results** is more than a framework. At its core, it reflects a philosophy rooted in human potential. Born from the field of Appreciative Inquiry.

SOAR emerged from the insight that individuals and organizations create more meaningful, lasting change when they focus on their strengths, past successes, and what gives them energy. This doesn't mean ignoring problems or sugarcoating reality. Instead, it acknowledges a fundamental truth about how the brain works: we move toward whatever we consistently focus on. When that focus is on strengths and possibilities, we're more likely to grow, thrive, and sustain change over time.

The real genius of SOAR lies in how it reshapes the entire coaching conversation. Rather than starting with "What's wrong and how do we fix it?", SOAR invites us to ask, "What's working and how do we amplify it?" This seemingly simple shift transforms more than just the questions we ask it changes how clients view themselves, what they believe is possible, and how they engage with change. When people operate from a place of strength, they experience more energy, creativity, and resilience. They begin to see themselves not as problems to solve, but as capable individuals with untapped potential. And through this lens, they build something essential: *self-efficacy*, the belief that they can rise to meet challenges and shape their own future. In the sections ahead, we'll walk through each phase of the SOAR model, exploring how this strengths-based approach turns everyday coaching into a powerful journey of personal growth and transformation.

So, how does it work in practice? Let's walk through the four phases of SOAR, one by one.

S – Strengths: Where It All Begins

This isn't about tossing around generic labels like "I'm good with people" or "I'm detail-oriented." It's deeper. It's about uncovering the unique ways a person thinks, feels, and acts that consistently lead to positive outcomes often without them even realizing it.

Truth is, most people are *blind* to their strengths. Not because they don't have them but because they've been trained to downplay them. They've been conditioned to focus on "areas of improvement." But let's face it you can't build a thriving life by obsessing over your flaws.

In SOAR, we do a bit of what we call **"appreciative archaeology."** We dig into past moments of success, joy, and impact not to create a polished highlight reel, but to find those recurring patterns of excellence. These aren't flukes. They're clues.

When exploring strengths, we're really looking at three layers:

1. **Natural talents** – Things that come so easily, they almost feel invisible to you.
2. **Developed strengths** – Skills and expertise you've sharpened over time.
3. **Character strengths** – Your values in action the inner compass guiding your behavior.

Try questions like:

- *"When do you feel most energized?"*
- *"What do people come to you for even when you don't advertise it?"*
- *"What challenge made you feel fully alive and confident?"*

And here's why it works: when we operate from strengths, our brain lights up. We activate well-worn neural pathways, creating that positive feedback loop of confidence → motivation → growth.

O – Opportunities: Seeing with New Eyes

Now, we zoom out.

This phase is about identifying external possibilities, but through the lens of our strengths and what truly matters to us. It's not about grabbing at every open door; it's about finding the ones that lead somewhere *you* actually want to go.

So many people approach opportunity with a scarcity mindset. They think, "I'm not ready," or "I'm not qualified." But in SOAR, we ask a better question, like

Where do your strengths meet a real-world need?

This is where **"appreciative scanning"** comes in. You start to see opportunities not as rare chances but as natural extensions of who you are.

Ask:

- *"Where is your unique way of working truly needed right now?"*
- *"What problems would you enjoy solving?"*
- *"What emerging trend makes you think, 'That's where I belong'?"*

You'll often find **adjacency opportunities**, possibilities sitting just beyond your current role or context but well within reach. And the best part? These aren't pipe dreams. They're grounded in your real capabilities and energy.

A – Aspirations: What Calls You Forward

This isn't about setting SMART goals or ticking boxes. It's about listening closely for what your soul is whispering to you.

Aspirations are different from goals. They're not externally imposed or socially expected. They're personal, magnetic, and deeply motivating. When your aspirations are aligned with your strengths and values, you don't need to push yourself toward them they *pull you forward*. But here's the thing many people confuse aspirations with pressure-filled "shoulds."

"I should get promoted."

"I'm supposed to start my own thing."

That's not aspiration. That's obligation in disguise.

In this phase, we do a bit of **"values archaeology."** We look at the through-lines of your life. What have you always cared about? What lights you up, even when no one's watching?

Try these:

- *"What legacy would you love to leave behind?"*
- *"What makes your heart ache and what gives you hope?"*
- *"If success were guaranteed, what would you attempt?"*

Neuroscience tells us that when your aspirations are internally driven aligned with your values and strengths you activate the brain's intrinsic motivation system. That's sustainable fuel. No burnout. No dragging yourself through.

R – Results: Bringing Vision to Life

Finally, we get practical, but in a very different way.

Most people think results require grit, hustle, and constant self-discipline. That's exhausting. And often unsustainable. SOAR flips that idea.

Instead of forcing yourself into rigid systems, this phase invites you to design *action* that flows with your natural energy and strengths. I call this **strength-based implementation.**

We begin with **"outcome visioning."** That means: What does success *feel* like? What's different in your life? Who are you becoming?

Then we ask:

- *"How will you know you're making progress?"*
- *"What first step would feel natural and energizing?"*
- *"What strengths will help you navigate the bumps?"*

The key here is **alignment.** When your actions reflect your strengths, aspirations, and values, results feel more like a natural extension of who you are not a constant uphill battle.

And it's never about getting it perfect. SOAR encourages **iterative implementation** taking a step, learning from it, and adjusting as you go. This creates momentum and keeps you connected to what truly matters.

You'll be amazed when you see what happens as all four elements of SOAR come together.

Each one Strengths, Opportunities, Aspirations, and Results is powerful on its own. But when they align? That's when transformation truly takes flight.

- **Strengths without Aspiration** = Comfort zone
- **Aspiration without Strengths** = Fantasy
- **Opportunity without Alignment** = Overwhelm
- **Results without Meaning** = Burnout

That's the *true* power of SOAR, it doesn't ask you to become someone else; it guides you to grow into the most **authentic**, **powerful**, and **purpose-driven** version of *yourself.*

It's not about striving harder. It's about aligning deeper with who you are, what matters to you, and what you're truly capable of when all the right pieces come together.

CHAPTER 13

Rewriting the Self: The Neuroscience of Narrative Identity Coaching

Let's Talk About Stories and Your Brain

Every human being has a story running in the background. Some of us carry stories of survival, some of resilience, some of invisibility, and some of being the fixer. These stories shape how we think, feel, decide and more importantly, how we show up.

And these stories aren't just psychological. They're neurobiological. Each time you revisit a thought about yourself ("I always get abandoned" or "I'm the reliable one"), your brain strengthens that neural pathway. Think of it like a well-worn trail in the forest it gets easier and easier to walk that route, even when it's not taking you where you want to go. But here's the empowering truth, the brain is rewritable. And stories can change. That's the essence of Narrative Identity Coaching.

What Is Narrative Identity Coaching?

Narrative Identity Coaching is a powerful approach that helps individuals explore the stories they tell about themselves and consciously re-author them. It's not therapy, and it's not just goal-setting. It sits beautifully in the space where insight meets forward movement. This coaching style integrates tools from neuroscience, positive psychology, and narrative therapy. Coaches listen for what's not said, gently challenge "fixed" identities, and help clients connect the dots between past experiences and present behaviors so they can begin writing the next chapter with intention.

In neuroscience terms, this is memory reconsolidation: when we revisit emotionally loaded memories in a safe environment, we can actually update them with new meaning. That means the story changes, and the brain physically changes with it.

Rewiring the Story Loop: A Brain-Based View

The science behind Narrative Identity Coaching is fascinating. Let's break it down...

- **Prefrontal Cortex Activation:** This part of your brain is responsible for self-reflection, planning, and identity formation. Engaging in narrative work strengthens its connectivity to emotional processing areas like the amygdala and hippocampus.
- **Neuroplasticity:** Telling your story differently fires different neurons. Repeat it with emotion and reflection, and the brain begins to *rewire*.
- **Dopamine & Motivation**: As clients visualize new identity possibilities, dopamine is released fueling motivation to act in line with the new story.
- **Cognitive Reappraisal:** By reframing painful memories, clients reduce emotional reactivity and increase psychological resilience.

Practical Tools for Narrative Identity Coaching

In the practice of Narrative Identity Coaching, it helps to anchor sessions around simple yet powerful techniques that allow clients to explore their inner world safely and constructively. These tools are not just interventions, they're invitations to rediscover the self with clarity and compassion. Below are three methods I frequently use to help clients reshape their narrative in ways that feel empowering and enduring.

1. Identity Theme Listening

This technique invites you, as a coach, to listen beyond the facts of a client's story. Pay close attention to how they *describe themselves*. The identity themes often emerge subtly through repeated phrases, emotional tone, or what they emphasize or omit.

Look out for roles or self-labels they consistently assume:

- Do they always frame themselves as the one who fixes everything?

- Do they downplay achievements with humor or self-doubt?
- Does their language carry tones of shame, defensiveness, or inflated pride?

Coach's Move: Gently mirror their language back to them. Then ask a pivotal question:

"Is that how you want your story to sound?"

This moment often sparks reflection, creating room for the client to pause and consider how their self-perception is shaping their reality.

2. Turning Point Mapping

We all carry a few defining moments that shape the arc of our identity sometimes consciously, other times without us even realizing their weight. In this technique, guide the client to identify 2–3 such pivotal events from their life. These can be moments of success, loss, betrayal, transition, or breakthrough.

Ask reflective questions such as:

- ***"What belief about yourself was formed here?"***
- ***"What decisions have you made since then because of that belief?"***

By connecting the emotional charge of the past with its influence on present-day behavior, you help clients see that their stories are *interpreted,* not fixed.

From there, invite them to expand their lens, "What else could you have learned from that experience?" This reframing activates meaning-making, resilience, and sometimes even forgiveness.

3. Story Re-authoring

Once a limiting narrative becomes visible, it's time to gently shift the client from *reporting the story* to *re-authoring it*. This is not about false optimism or rewriting history. It's about reclaiming agency and uncovering deeper truths that were perhaps buried under fear, failure, or habit.

Try using reflective, imaginative prompts like:

- *"If this story had a new title, what would it be?"*
- *"What strength or value was present in you even if it went unnoticed?"*
- *"If your future self could speak to you now, what would they say about this chapter?"*

This technique taps into self-compassion, growth mindset, and future orientation all key drivers of sustainable change.

Case Study: Rewriting the Story of "I'm Not Leadership Material"

Meet Neha. She's 36, a team lead in a growing tech company, and someone whose resume reads like a success story except she doesn't believe it. She came to coaching feeling "stuck" and unsure about applying for a promotion that would require managing a cross-functional team. Her words in the first session? *"I'm not leadership material. I just got lucky being here."*

As we explored her narrative, patterns emerged. Neha often downplayed her successes, attributed her wins to others, and described herself as someone who had to "hide" her real thoughts to fit in. Her core narrative wasn't about her abilities, it was about survival. Growing up in a family where her voice was often dismissed and where academic perfection was the only form of validation, Neha internalized the story: *"I'm valuable only when I don't make mistakes."*

Now here's the interesting bit from a neuroscience perspective: every time she recalled those formative moments, her brain's memory reconsolidation system was activating. This is the window of opportunity in coaching. The brain doesn't just store memory it updates it, especially when a new emotional insight is introduced alongside the memory. So instead of "fixing" her self-doubt, we worked with her story.

We identified a turning point: a project she led six years ago, during which she resolved a team conflict, delivered results under pressure, and even received a CEO award. But guess what? She never emotionally *owned* that moment. She had filed it under *"they didn't see the real me."*

In session, I asked:

a. "What if that award was not a fluke, but a data point in your leadership story?"

b. "If your younger self could see you today, what might she be surprised by?"

Over a few sessions, Neha began crafting a new narrative: *"I'm someone who leads quietly, with empathy and systems thinking. I've led in ways that didn't look like the textbook, but they worked. I'm allowed to define leadership on my terms."*

And here's where things shifted. Her language changed from avoidance to ownership. From "I can't" to "I'm learning." The final session? She had not only applied for the role but had already been shortlisted and more importantly, she *felt ready.*

Activity: Rewrite a Turning Point

Think of a moment in your life when something didn't go as expected like being overlooked, misunderstood, or doubting yourself after a setback. Now, give that memory a new title. One that reflects growth or insight. Write down what you learned about yourself through that moment, and what your future self might say to you about it now.

Try this as a journal entry titled: "The Story I'm Ready to Tell Differently."

CHAPTER 14

The Bridge Builder: An Ideal Self Journey

Once upon a time, in a quiet village between two hills, lived a man named Arjun. He was a skilled carpenter; known for his reliability and the sturdy homes he built. But deep inside, Arjun felt like something was missing. Every evening, he would climb the hill behind his house and look across the valley to the other hill where a beautiful golden light shimmered, calling to him.

People said that hill was magical. They called it the Hill of Becoming. It was said to be the place where a person could discover their truest self. But no one had ever gone there they were too afraid or too busy to try.

Arjun couldn't ignore the pull anymore. One morning, with only his tools and courage, he set out. But he quickly realized something: there was no path. Between him and the golden hill was a deep, misty valley. He couldn't jump across. He couldn't fly. If he wanted to reach it, he had to do what he knew best build a bridge. So he began. Each plank he laid came from something within him:

- One made of honesty, admitting what wasn't working.
- One made of courage, facing his fears of being "not enough."
- Another made of curiosity, exploring what truly mattered to him, not just what others expected.

Sometimes the wind howled. Sometimes the valley mocked him with fog and doubt. But every time he looked up at the golden light, he remembered why he started.

As days turned into seasons, Arjun's bridge grew longer and stronger. On that journey, he didn't just build outward he built inward. He discovered hidden strengths, old dreams buried under years of routine, and a voice inside that whispered, *"You're closer than you think."*

And one morning, after placing the final plank, he stepped onto the Hill of Becoming.

But to his surprise, the golden light wasn't something outside of him. It was coming from within him all along. He hadn't become someone new. He had simply met the version of himself he was always meant to be.

Moral: Your Ideal Self isn't across a distant land. It's on the other side of a bridge that only you can build with your truth, your values, and your will to grow.

The Architecture of Becoming

At the heart of personal growth lies a deep yearning: to become more aligned with our most valued, envisioned version of ourselves. In coaching, this transformative journey is often where the magic happens where reflection meets aspiration. Positive Psychology, with its focus on strengths, virtues, and potential, offers a powerful lens to navigate this path not through deficit correction, but through identity alignment.

Becoming your ideal self is not about erasing who you are it's about building on the foundation of your truth to express your highest potential. Picture a bridge: on one side stands your ***Actual Self,*** rooted in lived experience, habits, and identity. On the other side stands your ***Ideal Self*** the version of you that lives in alignment with your deepest values, aspirational traits, and purpose. The transformation lies not in jumping, but in constructing the bridge one intentional step at a time.

From a Positive Psychology lens, this bridge-building is a sacred process. It doesn't begin with what's broken, but with what's possible. It asks not, *"What's wrong with me?"* but *"What's strong within me?"* It's a dynamic dance between appreciating the now and aspiring for more not from inadequacy, but from inner calling.

This journey is less about self-improvement and more about self-activation awakening the parts of you that are authentic but perhaps under expressed. Positive Psychology emphasizes that human beings are not static; we are works in progress with the capacity for growth at every age and stage. The bridge between the actual and ideal self is not linear it's winding, reflective, and deeply personal. Each step forward requires courage, curiosity, and compassion toward the self that is still becoming.

Moreover, the process of becoming your ideal self is not a solitary pursuit. As you evolve, your relationships, work, and impact naturally shift to reflect this internal alignment. The bridge you build not only transforms your own life but serves as a guiding path for others. In this way, personal transformation becomes communal influence. Every step you take toward your ideal self creates a ripple that gives others silent permission to step into their own potential.

The Science Behind the Ideal Self

Psychologist Carl Rogers emphasized the importance of *congruence* the alignment between one's real self and ideal self as a foundational condition for psychological wellbeing. When this gap is too wide, individuals often experience internal conflict, low self-esteem, and phenomena like impostor syndrome. However, when this gap is narrowed not through perfection, but through mindful integration there is a notable increase in motivation, self-acceptance, and life satisfaction.

Positive Psychology builds on this concept by asking more generative questions:

- *What gives life meaning?*
- *What strengths already reside within you?*
- *What future version of yourself feels enlivening and purposeful?*

The "Ideal Self" is not a fantasy of flawless living it is a directional identity, a dynamic blueprint built from your values, aspirations, and innate potential. Rather than trying to become someone entirely new, the journey is about becoming more of who you already are on purpose.

This chapter introduces **The Ideal Self Compass,** a psychologically grounded, coaching-friendly model that equips individuals with tools to mindfully bridge the space between *"who I am"* and *"who I want to become."* Inspired by Positive Psychology, this compass doesn't just point toward a fixed destination; it helps navigate the evolving terrain of identity, values, and aspirations. It emphasizes three essential inner capacities: **clarity of vision** to define direction, **compassion for current reality** to stay grounded, and **conscious action** to walk the path ahead with intention and self-trust. Rather than pushing for perfection, The Ideal Self Compass guides individuals toward alignment so that who they are and who they are becoming move in graceful rhythm.

The Ideal Self Compass T

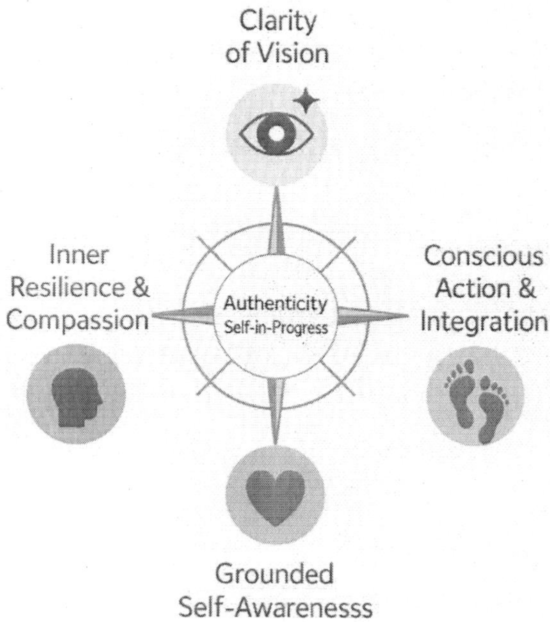

The Ideal Self Compass

A guiding tool to align identity, aspiration, and action

The compass consists of **four cardinal directions**, each representing a vital psychological capacity that supports the journey from Actual Self to Ideal Self.

North – Clarity of Vision

"Where am I headed?"

- Represents your **ideal self**, future aspirations, core values, and purpose.
- Encourages defining what a fulfilled, aligned life looks like.
- Uses visualization, strengths-spotting, and values clarification to set direction.
- In coaching: Use questions like "What does your best self-look like?" or "What kind of impact do you want to create?"

South – Grounded Self-Awareness

"Where am I now?"

- Symbolizes the **Actual Self**, including current habits, beliefs, roles, and lived experiences.
- Focuses on self-compassion, acceptance, and truth without judgment.
- Encourages awareness of inner narratives, strengths, and limiting patterns.
- In coaching: Use reflections like "What's working well right now?" and "What needs to be honored in your current reality?"

West – Inner Resilience & Compassion

"What sustains me on the journey?"

- Acts as the **emotional and psychological fuel** that helps individuals stay committed even in uncertainty.
- Emphasizes emotional regulation, self-kindness, and mindset work.
- Supports reframing setbacks and embracing progress over perfection.
- In coaching: Explore how clients treat themselves when things go wrong, and help build inner trust.

East – Conscious Action & Integration

"What am I ready to do?"

- Represents the movement forward action aligned with the ideal self.
- Encourages experimentation, habit-shaping, and micro-commitments.
- Invites clients to integrate their vision into everyday life with intention and flexibility.
- In coaching: Focus on goals, rituals, and accountability aligned with values.

Centre Point – Wholeness & Authenticity

At the center of the compass lies the **Self-in-Progress** the evolving, authentic being navigating life with intention. This symbolizes that you are never "behind" or "incomplete" you are simply *becoming*, guided by your own internal wisdom.

The *Ideal Self Compass* is not just a framework it's a living bridge between intention and transformation, for both coach and client. When coaches first use the compass for themselves, it becomes a self-reflective sanctuary a space to align their current path with their deeper calling. As they gain clarity on their own ideal self, they cultivate the empathy, presence, and grounded wisdom needed to walk alongside others. This internal alignment strengthens the coach's capacity to hold space not from a place of perfection, but from authentic becoming.

In turn, when shared with clients, the compass becomes a co-navigational tool. It invites meaningful dialogue around values, aspirations, and compassionate action. As coaches model the courage to engage with their own Ideal Self Compass, clients feel safer to explore their own. The coaching relationship transforms into a co-creative space, where both traveler and guide evolve. This is the essence of transformational coaching not instructing, but inspiring; not fixing, but facilitating the journey back to the truest self.

CHAPTER 15
Compassionate Navigation – Fueling the Journey with Self-Compassion and Flourishing Personas

When a client first encounters the *Ideal Self Compass,* the clarity it offers can feel both enlightening and overwhelming. Knowing who you want to become is empowering but it also exposes the gap between vision and current reality. It can stir a cocktail of emotions: excitement, fear, resistance, shame, even grief. At this intersection, the journey toward becoming the ideal self must be held gently, with tools not only for strategic alignment but also for **emotional navigation**.

This is where two powerful concepts from Positive Psychology and coaching converge: **Kristin Neff's Self-Compassion Model** and the practice of creating **Flourishing Personas**. Together, they help clients move forward not just with will, but with **warmth** bridging the internal gap between "I should be more" and "I am already becoming."

Why Compassion is Essential on the Path to Flourishing

Transformation is rarely linear. It's full of setbacks, detours, and moments where clients may feel like they're regressing rather than growing. In the absence of emotional resilience, these moments often become points of collapse. Many coaching journeys stall not because of lack of clarity or action, but because of **inner criticism** the subtle voice that says, "You're not enough," "You should have figured this out by now," or "Look at how far you still have to go."

Instead of treating these voices as enemies, **Self-Compassion** invites us to engage them as **misguided protectors**, offering outdated scripts that once served a purpose but now block growth. Dr. Kristin Neff's model offers a three-part reframe:

- **Self-Kindness over Self-Judgment**: Rather than pushing through with harshness, clients learn to meet themselves with patience and encouragement. Growth is allowed to be imperfect.
- **Common Humanity over Isolation**: Struggles aren't signs of failure they're part of the universal human experience. This realization creates a felt sense of belonging.
- **Mindfulness over Over-Identification**: Clients practice observing emotions with curiosity rather than becoming consumed by them. They pause, name their experience, and choose responses rather than react.

Incorporating self-compassion into coaching shifts the energy from fixing to healing and growing. It allows clients to take brave action from a place of wholeness, not deficiency.

"You can't shame yourself into growth. But you can love yourself into transformation."

The Coach as a Mirror of Compassion

When coaches embody self-compassion, they model what it looks like in tone, presence, and pacing. They normalize the messy middle of growth. They don't rush clients toward outcomes they hold space for discomfort, allow silence, validate setbacks, and gently invite reflection.

In practical terms, coaches can:

- Pause and check in with emotions before jumping to solutions.
- Reflect clients' efforts, not just achievements.
- Help clients name their inner critic and offer it a new role.
- Use affirming language: "You're exactly where you need to be to learn this next step."

By doing this, coaches create a **secure container** where clients don't just strategize but **heal and re-author their inner dialogue**.

Flourishing Personas - Bringing the Ideal Self to Life

Once clients have developed clarity through the *Ideal Self Compass* and emotional resilience through self-compassion, the next question emerges: *How do I live this out in real life?*

Enter the concept of **Flourishing Personas** an integrative coaching tool that helps clients consciously design the inner roles they want to play in various domains of life. Instead of being a fragmented self or a passive reactor to circumstances, the client becomes an **intentional leader of their life**, choosing how they want to show up in different roles.

What Are Flourishing Personas?

Flourishing Personas are intentional inner archetypes crafted, named, and embodied by the client to represent key qualities of their *Ideal Self* across different roles and life contexts. Unlike aspirational goals that feel distant or abstract, Flourishing Personas bring clarity and immediacy to personal growth by animating who the client wants to be, here and now.

They are not performances or personas adopted for approval they are authentic expressions of latent potential already residing within the individual. Each Flourishing Persona reflects not only desired traits but also a core purpose the client wishes to fulfill in a specific life domain.

Examples of Flourishing Personas

Domain	Persona Name	Key Traits	Empowering Affirmation
Work	The Strategic Visionary	Decisive, Insightful, Future-Focused	"I trust my ideas and lead with clarity."
Parenting	The Gentle Gardener	Present, Patient, Nurturing	"I create safe space for growth and love."
Relationships	The Brave Listener	Compassionate, Emotionally Honest, Attentive	"I meet others with openness and care."
Wellness	The Grounded Guardian	Consistent, Mindful, Disciplined	"I honor my body as a sacred foundation."
Creativity	The Wild Muse	Playful, Free-Spirited, Expressive	"I create with courage and delight."

These personas are not masks they are **intentional identities** that already live within the client, often underutilized. Through coaching, clients learn to **name**, **animate**, and **lead with** these personas, allowing different dimensions of their Ideal Self to express across life.

Why Use Flourishing Personas in Coaching?

Many clients struggle with vague goals like "I want to be more confident" or "I wish I handled things better." Flourishing Personas **translate these abstract ideals into embodied, actionable identities**. They provide:

- **Contextual Clarity**: Instead of one-size-fits-all change, clients create personas for different arenas leadership, relationships, self-care, creativity, etc.
- **Emotional Resonance**: Personas feel alive and memorable. They stir imagination and create emotional hooks for sustained practice.
- **Behavioral Anchoring**: With each persona, clients identify behaviors, mindsets, and language patterns they can activate in real-time.
- **Compassionate Self-Distancing**: In challenging moments, clients can ask "What would *The Brave Listener* do here?" a gentle way to respond rather than react.

Coaching Questions to Uncover Flourishing Personas

You can use these prompts to help clients discover and define their personas:

1. Who do you wish you could be in that part of your life?
2. What values do you want to express more in that space?
3. If that version of you had a title, nickname, or metaphor what would it be?
4. What would this part of you say, do, or believe differently?
5. When in your life have you *already* shown glimpses of this version?

Integration with the Ideal Self Compass

Flourishing Personas are not just imaginative exercises they are functional, directional tools within the broader *Ideal Self Compass* framework. Like the cardinal points of a compass, each persona offers orientation, alignment, and forward motion in specific areas of life.

- **North Star Vision**: Each persona helps the client personify the values and traits that define their aspirational self. The *Strategic Visionary* doesn't just want success they want *purposeful, values-aligned leadership*. Personas clarify what "becoming" really looks like in practice.
- **Self-Compassion as Fuel**: Embracing a new persona is not about perfection, but permission. Clients will falter, regress, or forget but that's expected. Through Kristen Neff's self-compassion lens, clients are reminded: "Even when I fall short, I can return to who I want to be with kindness and care."
- **Conscious Micro-Actions**: Personas translate insight into daily practice. Instead of abstract commitments, clients begin asking, *"What would The Brave Listener do in this conversation?"* or *"How would The Grounded Guardian end their day?"* This simple question becomes a habit loop that reorients behavior to purpose.

The *Ideal Self Compass* and *Flourishing Personas* are not just coaching frameworks they are living, breathing **acts of self-leadership**. Together, they empower individuals to bridge the gap between who they are and who they are capable of becoming not through pressure or pretense, but through mindful practice and soulful alignment.

For coaches, these tools offer a way to move beyond problem-fixing toward possibility-creating. For clients, they invite the joy of becoming **not just thinking differently, but being differently**. With time, consistency, and compassion, clients begin to experience themselves not as broken, but as *becoming*. And in that shift, true flourishing begins.

CHAPTER 16

Legacy-Driven Leadership – Coaching for Purpose Beyond Performance

As we approach the concluding chapters of this book, we shift our lens to a unique coaching audience **executives and leaders**. These individuals often operate in high-pressure environments where performance, deadlines, and bottom-line results dominate the narrative. However, beneath the pursuit of outcomes lies a deeper yearning: **the desire to be remembered for something meaningful**.

Leadership coaching at this level is not merely about strategic decisions or skill enhancement. It's about helping clients connect with their **Legacy** Self a future-facing identity rooted in values, impact, and contribution that goes beyond titles and KPIs. This chapter introduces a path to explore that legacy, starting with a powerful distinction.

Aryan stared at the quarterly report spread across his work desk. Every metric was green. Revenue up 23%. Team engagement scores at an all-time high. Customer satisfaction exceeding benchmarks. Yet as he closed her laptop that evening, a familiar emptiness settled in her chest.

"I'm winning at a game I'm not sure I want to play anymore," he confided during our first coaching session. Aryan's words capture what many high-achieving leaders experience: the growing disconnect between external performance and internal purpose. He mastered the "Performing Self" the version that delivers results and commands respect but lost touch with his "Legacy Self" the leader they truly want to become and be remembered for.

This chapter introduces one of the most transformative coaching approaches for executive leaders: helping them bridge the gap between performance and purpose.

Understanding the Two Selves

The Performing Self focuses primarily on measurable outcomes and KPIs, makes decisions based on immediate results, and derives identity from achievements. There's nothing wrong with this it's essential for success. The challenge arises when it becomes the only self that shows up in leadership.

The Legacy Self operates from deep purpose and values, makes decisions through the lens of long-term impact, and focuses on developing others while creating lasting positive change. The most impactful leaders integrate both selves, using performance as a vehicle for purpose rather than an end in itself.

The Eulogy vs. Resume Reflection: A Mirror for Authentic Leadership

What will they say when you're gone?

It's a question that startles even the most seasoned leaders into stillness not from fear of death, but from the quiet confrontation of a deeper truth:

That their calendars may be full, but their hearts may not be.

This coaching tool inspired by David Brooks' powerful distinction between résumé virtues (skills that get you hired) and eulogy virtues (qualities you want remembered) acts as a mirror for the soul. It brings into focus what lies behind the curtain of success.

Leaders often spend decades crafting a story that earns applause but deep down, many wonder:

"Is this the story I truly want to be remembered for?"

Step 1: The Resume – Crafting the Outer Narrative

Start by inviting your client to write their professional résumé:

- Titles held
- Projects delivered
- Revenues driven

- Awards won
- Promotions achieved

Let them fill the page with what they've worked tirelessly to earn. This list represents their performing self how the external world measures success.

Then pause. Now, invite a shift.

Not upward or forward but inward.

Step 2: The Eulogy – Writing the Inner Legacy

Ask them to switch lenses and envision a future memorial.

"Imagine it's 7 years from now," you might say.

"Your colleagues, mentees, family, and friends have gathered to speak about your life. What do you hope they say?"

Prompt them to reflect on qualities beyond performance, such as:

- "She made people feel safe."
- "He stood up for what mattered."
- "They always brought out the best in others."
- "She lived her values unapologetically."

This exercise is not about mortality. It's about immortality what lives on in others because of who you chose to be.

Step 3: Holding the Mirror – Coaching the Dissonance

Now place the résumé and eulogy side by side.

Let the client look into the mirror of their life.

Ask gently:

- "What's missing from your eulogy that your current reality doesn't reflect yet?"
- "Which parts of your résumé feel like obligations, not expressions of you?"
- "Where do performance and purpose overlap and where do they conflict?"

This moment of dissonance becomes fertile ground for clarity.

It is not a judgment it's a mirror of alignment.

What Coaches Should Notice:

- Emotional cues: A pause. A distant gaze. A tremble in the voice. These signal contact with something true.
- Defensive explanations: "But I had to do that to succeed." Explore this with care it often reveals the tension between survival and self.
- Longing statements: "I've always wanted to..." These are breadcrumbs. Follow them.

Why This Reflection Works

This tool doesn't ask leaders to **reject** performance.

It invites them to **redefine** it.

By anchoring achievement to authenticity, clients learn to lead with both results **and** resonance. They discover they don't have to choose between credibility and character. They can become leaders who **inspire, not just instruct** who **leave a legacy**, not just a title.

Example Dialogue

Coach: "Looking at both, what surprised you the most?"

Client *(softly)*: "I never realized how little of what truly matters shows up in my résumé... and yet, it's what I most want to be known for."

Coach: "What's one micro-action this week that moves you toward your eulogy self?"

The Eulogy vs. Résumé Reflection is not a performance evaluation.

It is a values alignment mirror an invitation to lead from the inside out.

As coaches, our role is to hold that mirror gently, and ask:

"Who are you becoming and who do you choose to be remembered as?"

Case Study: The Transformation of Danid Chen

Danid Chen, VP of Operations at a Fortune 500 technology company, consistently delivered exceptional results. His teams hit every deadline; his processes were models of efficiency. Yet at 45, he questioned everything: "I've spent 20 years climbing this mountain, and I'm starting to wonder if it's the right mountain."

Through the Eulogy vs. Resume exercise, Danid realized the gap between his achievements and his aspirations. His purpose mapping revealed core values of Excellence, Mentorship, Innovation, and Authentic Leadership, leading to his impact vision: "To be a leader who proves that driving results and developing people aren't competing priorities they're synergistic ones."

Danid implemented key changes: shifting one-on-ones from status updates to growth-focused dialogues, creating innovation mentorship programs for junior staff, leading with vulnerability and transparency, and making values-based decisions.

Six months later, his division saw 35% increased engagement scores, doubled internal promotion rates, improved customer satisfaction, and exceeded performance targets all while maintaining higher team satisfaction. Most significantly, Danid experienced profound personal transformation: "I'm working harder than ever, but it doesn't feel like work anymore."

Values-Driven Visioning

Traditional strategic planning starts with market analysis. Values-driven visioning begins with purpose and values, then builds strategy that serves deeper intention using the Three-Horizon Framework:

Horizon 1 (6-12 months): How can we excel at current responsibilities while staying true to our values?

Horizon 2 (1-3 years): What initiatives would advance both performance and purpose?

Horizon 3 (5-10 years): What would success look like if we stayed true to our deepest values?

These shifts planning questions from "How can we increase revenue?" to "How can we grow in a way that reflects our values?" and "What would our stakeholders say about the kind of organization we're becoming?"

Legacy-driven leadership isn't a sentimental ideal it's a strategic shift in how leaders see themselves, their teams, and their impact. When leaders begin to operate from a space of deep purpose and anchored values, it doesn't just elevate their decision-making. It begins to ripple outward. Conversations become more meaningful. Priorities shift toward what matters most. Teams start asking different questions, not just about tasks, but about meaning, motivation, and contribution.

This ripple effect is what makes legacy coaching so potent. It moves beyond short-term wins and shapes long-term transformation. Cultures evolve. Trust deepens. Innovation thrives because people feel seen, valued, and connected to something bigger than performance metrics.

Yet, this transformation doesn't come without tension.

As a coach, your most vital role is supporting the integration of the Performing Self with the Legacy Self. Help your clients hold space for complexity: the boardroom demands and the heart's longing, the urgent deliverables and the timeless values, the pressure to win and the desire to matter.

Support them as they navigate:

- Leading with values when KPIs falter.
- Staying true to self while adapting to context.
- Driving results while allowing purpose to unfold slowly.
- Extending influence beyond success to significance.

Leadership doesn't stop at outcomes. It matures into legacy when leaders realize that who they become is their most enduring achievement.

And this is where coaching becomes truly transformational. You're not just helping your clients lead more effectively. You're helping them become leaders worth following, worth remembering, and ultimately, leaders who can look at both their résumé and their eulogy and say, "That's the life I meant to live."

CHAPTER 17

The Leader's Mindset – From Fixed Patterns to Growth Pathways

Leadership begins in the mind long before it's expressed in action or decision-making. At the center of every effective leader is a relationship with discomfort: the discomfort of uncertainty, of making mistakes, of being seen trying. The way a leader responds to these moments reveals not just their personality, but their mindset an internal framework that quietly shapes everything.

At its core, mindset is the belief system that governs how you interpret challenges. According to **Dr. Carol Dweck**, there are two major types:

Fixed Mindset	**Growth Mindset**
"I'm either good at this or I'm not."	"I can get better with practice."
Avoids challenges	Seeks challenges
Sees feedback as personal	Sees feedback as fuel
Effort = weakness	Effort = growth process
Threatened by others' success	Inspired by others' success

Some leaders operate from a fixed pattern of thinking. They carry the belief often unspoken that ability is static. Intelligence is what you were born with. Charisma, chutzpah, decisiveness, resilience either you have them, or you don't. In this state of mind, challenges feel like threats, not invitations. Feedback feels like a judgment, not an opportunity. The response to failure becomes avoidance or blame, rather than reflection or recalibration.

But the human brain is not wired to be fixed. In fact, it is inherently built to adapt. Every time a person attempts something difficult, reflects on an error, or changes the way they interpret an experience, the brain makes new connections. These are not motivational slogans. They are structural changes happening inside the brain. This is the power of neuroplasticity the biological truth that change is possible through repeated mental effort and attention.

Growth-oriented leaders begin to notice their internal language. They might catch themselves saying, "I'm just not good at strategy," or "I've never been great with people," and pause. In that pause, something different begins to happen. The brain, when given even a small window of awareness, begins to open. Instead of rehearsing failure, it starts building readiness.

This doesn't mean forcing positivity or pretending struggle doesn't exist. It means staying curious in the presence of discomfort. When a project fails, a growth mindset doesn't ask, "Why am I like this?" It asks, "What patterns can I now see?" The brain, when trained this way, becomes less reactive. It learns to process ambiguity without collapsing into helplessness.

Effort plays a central role here. Not all effort is equal. Passion may get a leader started, but it's consistency daily, sometimes unglamorous action that tells the brain this direction matters. Every time a leader leans into a hard conversation, plans instead of avoids, or sits with uncomfortable feedback without needing to defend, the brain rewards that focus. Not through external success, but through internal reinforcement. Over time, the path of persistence becomes the brain's preferred route.

This is not about becoming perfect or endlessly driven. It's about making it easier to choose growth when it would be simpler to shut down. Just like muscles adapt to training, the mind becomes more flexible, more focused, and more capable of leading under pressure when it's exercised consistently in the direction of learning.

Leaders who embrace this way of thinking don't rely on motivation. They build rhythm. They understand that growth often begins where motivation ends. They show up, not because it feels good, but because it rewires who they are becoming. They don't chase ease; they develop endurance. And in doing so, they become not just better leaders but more integrated, aware versions of themselves.

Growth, in this view, isn't an achievement. It's a biological process, a mental discipline, and a deeply human way to meet the world.

Real transformation doesn't occur through insight alone. Awareness must meet action. In coaching, once a leader begins to recognize their mindset patterns, the next step is to convert those insights into lived, repeatable experiences. This is where structure becomes useful not to impose rigidity, but to offer rhythm. A good framework in coaching serves as scaffolding. It holds space while new neural and behavioral habits are being formed.

One such approach involves guiding the leader through three layers of reflection: **Notice, Name, Navigate.** While simple on the surface, each layer works with how the brain processes change.

- **Notice** is about building awareness. The leader begins to observe their recurring mental patterns. This could include self-limiting thoughts during high-stakes meetings, hesitations in delegating, or emotional spikes in response to criticism. Awareness itself starts creating distance between reaction and response, an essential shift from automatic behavior to conscious choice.
- **Name** brings language into the picture. Neuroscience confirms that labelling an emotion or thought reduces its intensity. When a leader can say, "This is my pattern of assuming I'm not ready," or "This is me equating effort with failure," they engage the prefrontal cortex, which helps regulate emotional reactivity. Naming also supports accountability; once something is spoken, it can be worked with.
- **Navigate** is where forward movement begins. Instead of aiming for perfection, the leader considers what one action, one new behavior, or one new interpretation is possible. The goal is not to fix the problem immediately, but to disrupt the pattern gently and consistently.

This reflection framework can be practiced through short weekly coaching check-ins. A leader might bring a challenge they faced and walk through this structure. Over time, they begin using the framework on their own. It becomes internalized not as a formula, but as a way of relating to difficult experiences more adaptively.

To deepen the process, coaches can introduce a **practice tool** that builds neuro-muscular memory of effort and attention

One such practice involves a "**Deliberate Discomfort Rehearsal.**" It's a simple yet powerful routine where the leader identifies one action, they tend to avoid like giving difficult feedback, presenting without over-preparing, or asking for help and deliberately schedules that behavior in the coming week. The intention is not to succeed at it perfectly, but to *show up for it*. This act of showing up, especially in small and manageable doses, creates familiarity in the brain. What was once threatening becomes tolerable. Eventually, it becomes integrated.

Worksheet: Deliberate Discomfort Rehearsal

Purpose: To build emotional resilience and adaptability by intentionally engaging in avoided leadership behaviors.

STEP 1: Identify the Avoided Action

Reflect on a leadership behavior you often resist due to fear, discomfort, or overthinking.

Examples:

- ☐ Giving candid feedback
- ☐ Asking for help or clarity
- ☐ Presenting without over-preparing
- ☐ Delegating without micromanaging
- ☐ Saying "no" to a non-essential task
- ☐ Other: ______________________________

What behavior do I avoid because it feels uncomfortable or exposing?

____

____

STEP 2: Schedule the Rehearsal

Choose **one** avoided action from above and schedule it for the coming week.

- **What will I do?**
  ____
- **When and where will I do it?**
  Date: __________ Time: __________ Context: ______________
- **How will I know I showed up for it?**
  ____

STEP 3: Show Up Mindfully

Before the Action:

☐ Take 3 slow, deep breaths

☐ Acknowledge fear or resistance without judgment

☐ Remind yourself: *"The goal is to practice, not to perfect."*

During the Action:

☐ Stay present

☐ Focus on *doing*, not *proving*

☐ Be aware of internal shifts

STEP 4: Reflect After the Action

Write your responses:

1. **What did I feel before, during, and after?**

   ____

   ____

2. **What did my brain predict would happen?**

   ____

3. **What actually happened?**

   ____

4. **What did I learn about myself?**

   ____

5. **What will I do differently next time?**

   ____

This reflection helps close the loop between discomfort, action, and growth.

Weekly Intention Tracker

Week	Action Rehearsed	Showed Up	Key Insight or Takeaway

Tip: Repeat this exercise weekly to strengthen your tolerance for discomfort and embed adaptive behaviors into your leadership identity.

What makes this tool effective is the loop of feedback. After the action, the leader reflects not only on the outcome but on their own internal response. How did they feel before, during, and after? What did the brain predict, and what actually happened? This closes the loop between fear, effort, and reward strengthening the belief that growth is possible and effort is worthwhile.

Mindset is not a motivational idea it is a biological reality. What we choose to focus on, how we interpret discomfort, and how we respond to challenge quite literally shapes the architecture of our brain. As leaders, our ability to grow begins with how we see ourselves in moments of pressure, uncertainty, or doubt.

CHAPTER 18

Strengths-Shadow Dialogue Harnessing the Light Without Getting Burned

"Your strength overplayed can become your greatest liability." – *Robert E. Kaplan*

As a coach, you'll meet clients from diverse walks of life leaders, professionals, entrepreneurs, creatives, and even those in transition. Each person carries a unique blend of strengths. Yet, what often goes unnoticed is how these very strengths, when overused or unconsciously applied, can become obstacles.

This chapter, is your practical guide to understanding and managing the **duality of strengths** the brilliance and the blind spots. Whether you're coaching someone highly driven, deeply empathetic, overly structured, or excessively adaptable, the examples and tools will help you recognize when their strengths serve them and when those strengths start working against them.

The goal here is twofold:

1. To help you spot subtle patterns that even your clients may not be aware of.
2. To equip your clients with a **self-awareness system** they can use long after the session ends.

Throughout this chapter, you'll find **structured reflection prompts**, early **warning signals**, **used cases** and **realignment tools** designed to meet the needs of professionals across different industries.

Whether your client is:

- A corporate leader struggling with over-control,
- A caregiver overwhelmed by their giving nature,
- A young achiever burning out from perfectionism...this navigator can be customized and applied with ease.

The brilliance is already within your client. This chapter helps ensure **they don't burn out in their own light.**

Our Journey Starts By!

Introduction: The Paradox of Excellence

Rachel was the kind of leader everyone wanted on their team. Her empathy was legendary she could read a room, sense when someone was struggling, and offer exactly the right words of support. For years, this strength had propelled her career forward, earning her promotions and the deep loyalty of her teams. But when she called me for coaching, she was exhausted, overwhelmed, and questioning everything she thought she knew about leadership.

"I don't understand," she said during our first session. "I'm doing everything I've always done caring for my people, being there for them, making sure everyone feels heard. But somehow, it's all falling apart. My team seems dependent on me for everything, I'm working sixteen-hour days, and my boss says I need to be more strategic. How can caring too much be a problem?"

Rachel had discovered one of the most counterintuitive truths in human development: our greatest strengths, when taken to extremes, can become our most significant liabilities. She wasn't failing because she lacked empathy she was struggling because her empathy had gone into overdrive, creating a cascade of unintended consequences that were undermining her effectiveness and well-being.

This phenomenon, the "**strengths-shadow dialogue,**" is at the heart of why so many talented individuals plateau in their careers, why high-performing teams sometimes implode, and why personal development work can feel like a frustrating cycle of two steps forward, one step back. Understanding this dialogue and learning to navigate it skillfully is perhaps the most crucial skill for anyone seeking to maximize their potential while maintaining their authenticity.

The Mirror and the Spotlight: Understanding the Duality

The Flashlight Analogy

Imagine you're hiking on a moonless night with only a powerful flashlight to guide you. In the darkness, this tool is invaluable. It illuminates the path ahead, reveals potential hazards, and gives you the confidence to keep moving forward. The brighter the beam, the better you can see, and the faster you can travel.

But what happens when you encounter another hiker? If you keep that powerful beam pointed directly at them, what was once helpful becomes harmful. The light that guided you now blinds them. They can't see where they're going, they stumble, and they might even become irritated or hostile toward you. Your greatest asset in the darkness has become a barrier to connection and collaboration.

This is precisely how our strengths operate in the complex social and professional environments we navigate daily. In the right context, applied with the right intensity, they're our superpowers. But context is everything, and intensity matters more than we often realize.

The Neuroscience of Strength Overuse

Recent research in neuroscience helps explain why we're prone to overusing our strengths. Our brains are pattern-recognition machines, constantly seeking efficiency through repetition and automation. When we discover something we're good at that brings us success, recognition, or satisfaction our neural pathways strengthen around that behavior.

Dr. Rick Hanson, a neuropsychologist, describes this as the brain's tendency to "take the shape of what the mind rests upon." If we repeatedly rely on a particular strength, our brains literally restructure themselves to make that strength more accessible and automatic. This is wonderful for building expertise, but it can also create what neuroscientists call "cognitive rigidity" an unconscious bias toward applying familiar solutions even when the situation calls for something different.

Consider David, a brilliant analytical thinker who rose through the ranks of his consulting firm by consistently delivering data-driven insights that solved complex problems. His ability to break down complicated issues into logical components was extraordinary. However, when he was promoted to lead a team tasked with innovation and creative problem-solving, his analytical strength became a liability. His instinct to immediately dissect and critique new ideas was shutting down the very creativity his team needed to succeed.

The neural pathways that had made David successful were now working against him, but his brain couldn't distinguish between helpful and harmful applications of his strength. Without conscious intervention, he would continue to default to analysis, wondering why his new role felt so much more difficult than his previous ones.

The Cultural Amplification Effect

Our tendency to overuse strengths is further amplified by cultural and organizational factors. Most cultures have implicit hierarchies of valued traits think of how Western business culture tends to reward assertiveness, speed, and decisive action, while sometimes undervaluing reflection, collaboration, and patience.

When our natural strengths align with culturally valued traits, we receive consistent positive reinforcement that encourages us to lean even more heavily into those strengths. We get promoted, praised, and positioned as role models, which creates a feedback loop that can gradually push our strengths into overdrive.

Maya, a naturally decisive executive, thrived in a fast-paced startup environment where quick decisions were essential for survival. Her ability to rapidly process information and make firm choices saved the company countless hours and helped them out maneuver larger competitors. However, as the company grew and decisions became more complex, requiring input from diverse stakeholders, Maya's strength began to backfire. Her speed, once an asset, was now perceived as recklessness. Her decisiveness, once celebrated, was now seen as autocratic.

The culture that had initially rewarded her strength had evolved, but Maya's neural patterns and self-concept hadn't adapted accordingly. She was still applying startup-speed decision-making to enterprise-complexity problems, creating friction and resistance throughout the organization.

The Psychological Foundation: Jung's Shadow and Modern Strengths Research

Beyond the Traditional Shadow

Carl Jung's concept of the shadow traditionally focused on the repressed, denied, or undeveloped aspects of personality, the parts of ourselves we'd rather not acknowledge. But Jung also recognized that the shadow could include positive qualities that become problematic through excess or misapplication.

In his later writings, Jung observed that "the most terrifying thing is to accept oneself completely," partly because this acceptance must include recognition of how our virtues can become vices. He noted that individuals often become so identified with their strengths that they lose the ability to see when those strengths are no longer serving them or others.

This insight has profound implications for personal development. Traditional approaches often focus on identifying and building strengths while separately addressing weaknesses. But the shadow-strengths perspective suggests that our development challenges are often not about lacking certain qualities, but about being unconscious of how our existing qualities are showing up in the world.

The Aristotelian Mean Applied to Strengths

Aristotle's concept of the "Golden Mean," the idea that virtue lies between extremes, provides another lens for understanding the strengths-shadow dynamic. Aristotle stated that qualities like courage, generosity, and confidence become virtues only when applied in the right amount, at the right time, in the right context. Too little courage becomes cowardice; too much becomes recklessness.

Modern strengths research has validated this ancient wisdom. Studies by researchers like Robert Biswas-Diener have shown that character strengths follow an inverted U-curve: performance and well-being increase as we develop and apply our strengths, but only up to a point. Beyond that optimal level, continued increase in strength usage actually decreases effectiveness and satisfaction.

This research challenges the popular notion that "more is always better" when it comes to strengths. Instead, it suggests that wisdom lies in developing what we might call "strengths intelligence "the ability to modulate our strengths based on contextual demands.

The Overuse Research: When Strengths Become Liabilities

Dr. Robert Kaiser's extensive research on leadership derailment has identified overused strengths as one of the primary causes of executive failure. His studies of hundreds of leaders found that successful executives don't just have strong capabilities, they have the ability to flex those capabilities up or down based on situational requirements.

Dr. Kaiser's research revealed several key patterns:

The Intensity Trap: High-performing individuals often believe that if a moderate application of a strength works well, then maximum application will work even better. This logic fails because it ignores the complex, non-linear relationship between strength intensity and effectiveness.

The Success Trap: Past success with a particular approach creates confidence and commitment to that approach, making individuals less likely to notice when circumstances have changed and a different response is needed.

The Identity Trap: When we become too identified with our strengths, questioning their application feels like questioning our core identity. This psychological investment makes it difficult to receive feedback about overuse and even harder to experiment with alternative approaches.

Neuroplasticity and the Possibility of Change

The good news emerging from neuroscience research is that our brains remain remarkably plastic throughout our lives. The same neural mechanisms that can lock us into overused strength patterns can also help us develop more flexible, contextually appropriate responses.

Dr. Daniel Siegel's research on "mindsight" the ability to see the internal world of self and others shows that conscious awareness can literally reshape our neural architecture. When we become mindful of our automatic strength patterns, we create space for choice, and choice creates the possibility for new neural pathways to develop.

This means that the tendency to overuse strengths isn't a fixed personality trait it's a changeable pattern that can be modified through awareness and practice. The key is developing what I call "strengths metacognition" the ability to think about how we're thinking about and applying our strengths.

The Spectrum of Strength Expression: From Shadow to Brilliance

Understanding the Continuum

Rather than thinking of strengths as simply "on" or "off," it's more helpful to visualize them as existing on a continuum from underuse through optimal use to overuse. Each point on this continuum produces different outcomes and requires different developmental approaches.

Underuse (The Dimmer Switch) When we underuse our strengths, we're like someone with a dimmer switch turned too low. We have the capability, but we're not accessing it fully. This might happen due to:

- Lack of confidence or self-awareness
- Cultural or organizational constraints
- Past negative experiences that created hesitation
- Inability to discern when the strength is appropritate

Consider Jennifer, a naturally gifted strategic thinker who consistently underused this strength in her role as a project manager. She had learned to focus on tactical execution and was so busy managing details that she rarely stepped back to question whether the projects themselves were aligned with broader organizational goals. When she finally began to apply her strategic thinking more fully, both her satisfaction and her value to the organization increased dramatically.

Optimal Use (The Sweet Spot) Optimal strength use occurs when we apply the right amount of a strength at the right time in the right context. This requires:

- Contextual awareness
- Emotional regulation
- Flexibility in application
- Integration with other strengths and capabilities

Marcus, a sales leader with strong relationship-building abilities, exemplified optimal strength use. He could dial up his warmth and connection when meeting new prospects, maintain appropriate boundaries when negotiating contracts, and shift to a more challenging, coach-like approach when developing his team members. His strength wasn't constant it was contextually intelligent.

Overuse (The Blinding Light) Overuse occurs when we apply too much of a strength, apply it inappropriately, or rely on it exclusively when other approaches might be more effective. Signs of overuse include:

- Diminishing returns despite increased effort
- Negative feedback about behaviors we consider positive
- Feeling stuck or frustrated despite using our "best" qualities
- Others seem resistant or disengaged when we apply our strengths

The Shadow Expressions: How Strengths Go Dark

Each strength has predictable shadow expressions that emerge when it moves into overuse. Understanding these patterns can help us recognize when we're crossing the line from helpful to harmful.

Empathy → Enmeshment Healthy empathy allows us to understand and connect with others' experiences while maintaining appropriate boundaries. Shadow empathy becomes enmeshment taking on others' emotions as our own, becoming over-responsible for others' feelings, and losing our own emotional center in the process.

Lisa, a team leader with strong empathic abilities, found herself constantly stressed and overwhelmed because she was emotionally absorbing every challenge and conflict her team members faced. Her intention to be supportive had evolved into an unhealthy pattern where she felt responsible for managing everyone else's emotional state. This not only exhausted her but also prevented her team members from developing their own emotional resilience.

Confidence → Arrogance Healthy confidence involves appropriate self-assurance and belief in one's abilities. Shadow confidence becomes arrogance, dismissing others' perspectives, failing to recognize limitations, and believing that confidence alone is sufficient for success.

Alex was a brilliant software architect whose technical confidence had served him well early in his career. However, as he moved into leadership roles, his confidence began to manifest as arrogance. He would dismiss teammates' suggestions without proper consideration, make unilateral decisions in areas where he lacked expertise, and respond defensively to any questioning of his approaches. His confidence, once an asset, was now creating team dysfunction and limiting innovation.

Drive → Drivenness Healthy drive provides motivation and energy for pursuing important goals. Shadow drive becomes drivenness, compulsive action without sufficient reflection, inability to rest or celebrate success, and pushing others beyond their sustainable capacity.

Raphael was a marketing executive whose natural drive had helped her build a successful career. However, when she was promoted to lead a larger team, her drive went into overdrive. She began setting unrealistic deadlines, working weekends consistently, and expecting the same level of intensity from everyone around her. Her drivenness was creating burnout throughout her organization and actually decreasing overall productivity due to turnover and mistakes caused by rushing.

Analytical Thinking → Analysis Paralysis Healthy analytical thinking involves gathering relevant information and thinking through problems systematically. Shadow analytical thinking becomes analysis paralysis over-researching, endlessly seeking more data, and being unable to make decisions with incomplete information.

Tom was a strategic planner whose analytical abilities were renowned throughout his organization. However, when faced with a rapidly changing market situation, his analytical strength became a liability. He kept requesting more studies, more data, and more analysis while competitors were taking action. His team became frustrated with the endless research cycles, and opportunities were lost while he continued to analyze.

The Contextual Nature of Shadows

One of the most important insights about strength shadows is that they're highly contextual. A behavior that's perfectly appropriate in one situation can be completely inappropriate in another. This means that developing strong intelligence requires not just self-awareness, but also contextual awareness.

Consider the strength of assertiveness:

- In crisis situations requiring quick decisions, leaders might need to dial up their assertiveness in brainstorming sessions, **excessive assertiveness** can stifle creative input, so a more **receptive approach** may be needed. In a performance management conversation, assertiveness might need to be balanced with empathy
- In a client presentation, assertiveness might need to be combined with adaptability

The same individual might need to express their assertiveness very differently across these contexts, sometimes within the same day or even the same meeting.

The Individual's Journey: Working with Strengths Consciously

Phase 1: Recognition – Developing Strengths Awareness

The journey toward conscious strength use begins with developing comprehensive awareness of how our strengths actually show up in the world, not just how we think they show up or how we intend them to show up.

Tools for Self-Assessment While assessments like VIA Character Strengths, CliftonStrengths, and the Enneagram can provide valuable starting points, they're most useful when combined with real-world observation and feedback. The most effective approach involves multiple data sources:

360-Degree Feedback: Gathering input from supervisors, peers, direct reports, and even clients about how your strengths are perceived and experienced by others.

***Behavioral Tracking*:** Keeping a daily log for several weeks, noting when you use specific strengths, the context, and the outcomes.

***Video Review*:** Recording yourself in various professional situations (with appropriate permissions) and reviewing the recordings to observe your strength patterns objectively.

***Critical Incident Analysis*:** Examining specific moments when your strengths either served you exceptionally well or seemed to backfire, looking for patterns and contextual factors.

Phase 2: Calibration – Understanding Context and Dosage

Once we develop awareness of our strength patterns, the next phase involves learning to calibrate our strengths based on contextual demands. This requires developing what I call "situational intelligence"- the ability to read situations accurately and adjust our approach accordingly.

The CONTEXT Framework To develop better situational intelligence, consider these contextual factors:

Culture: What are the explicit and implicit norms of this environment? What strengths are valued, discouraged, or misunderstood here?

Others: Who else is involved, and what are their needs, preferences, and current states? How might they receive your strengths?

Nature of the task: What is actually required for success in this situation? What strengths are most relevant?

Timing: What's the pace and urgency level? Is this a time for quick action or careful deliberation?

Emotional climate: What's the emotional tone of the situation? Are people stressed, excited, uncertain, or focused?

Xpectations: What are the explicit and implicit expectations for behavior in this context?

Tracks record: What has worked or not worked in similar situations in the past?

For example, James was a naturally collaborative leader who excelled at building consensus and ensuring everyone felt included in decisions. However, he learned to calibrate this strength differently based on context:

- In strategic planning sessions, he would dial up his collaborative approach, ensuring all perspectives were heard before making decisions
- In crisis situations, he would dial down collaboration in favor of more directive leadership, making quick decisions and communicating them clearly
- In one-on-one coaching conversations, he would balance collaboration with appropriate challenge, knowing when to push and when to support

Developing Dosage Control Like medication, strengths are most effective when applied in appropriate dosages. Too little has no impact; too much can be toxic. Developing dosage control requires:

Experimentation: Deliberately trying different intensity levels of your strengths in various situations and observing the results.

Feedback Loops: Creating systems for getting real-time feedback about how your strengths are being received.

Self-Monitoring: Developing internal awareness of your energy levels, emotional states, and effectiveness when using different strength intensities.

Pause Practices: Building in moments of reflection before automatically applying your strengths, asking questions like "What's needed here?" and "How much of this strength is appropriate?"

Phase 3: Integration – Developing Strengths Flexibility

The third phase involves integrating our strengths with other capabilities and developing the flexibility to access different strengths as situations require. This is perhaps the most sophisticated aspect of strengths development and often requires support from coaches, mentors, or developmental programs.

Building Complementary Capabilities Rather than trying to develop strengths we don't naturally possess, it's often more effective to build complementary capabilities that can balance our dominant strengths. This might involve:

Partnering: Collaborating with others whose strengths complement our own *Skill Development*: Learning specific techniques or frameworks that provide structure for applying non-dominant strengths *Mindset Shifts*: Adopting different mental models or perspectives that naturally activate different strengths

For instance, David, the analytical leader mentioned earlier, didn't try to become naturally creative. Instead, he learned specific facilitation techniques that helped him create space for others' creativity while still contributing his analytical perspective when appropriate.

The Integration Challenge Integration is challenging because it requires us to hold multiple, sometimes contradictory approaches simultaneously. A leader might need to be both supportive and challenging, both decisive and collaborative, both confident and humble sometimes within the same conversation.

This level of sophistication requires what developmental psychologists call "dialectical thinking" the ability to hold tension between opposing forces rather than resolving them prematurely. It's a key characteristic of what Robert Kegan calls "self-transforming mind," the highest level of adult development.

Personal Strengths Philosophy As individuals develop greater sophistication in working with their strengths, many find it helpful to articulate a personal strengths philosophy, a set of principles that guide how they think about and apply their capabilities. This might include:

- Core values that inform strength application
- Personal mission or purpose that provides direction for strength use
- Principles for balancing competing demands or strengths
- Guidelines for when to push beyond comfort zones and when to stay within them
- Commitments to ongoing learning and development

Elena, a senior executive with strong visionary abilities, developed this personal strength's philosophy: "I use my vision to inspire possibility while staying grounded in practical reality. I share my vision in ways that invite others to contribute rather than demanding compliance. I regularly test my vision against data and feedback, remaining open to course corrections while maintaining confidence in the overall direction."

The Coach's Art: Facilitating the Strengths-Shadow Dialogue

The Coach as Mirror: Reflecting Reality with Compassion

One of the most crucial roles a coach plays in strengths development is serving as a high-quality mirror reflecting to clients how their strengths are actually showing up in the world, not just how they intend them to show up. This requires a delicate balance of honesty and compassion, challenge and support.

Creating Psychological Safety for Shadow Exploration Before clients can explore the shadow sides of their strengths, they need to feel psychologically safe. This means creating an environment where:

- Shadows are normalized as natural and universal rather than shameful
- The focus is on growth and effectiveness rather than judgment
- Mistakes and overuse are treated as valuable learning opportunities
- The client's essential worth and capability are never questioned, even when specific behaviors are challenged

Supra, the empathetic leader from our opening story, initially became defensive when her coach suggested that her caring might be contributing to her team's over-dependence. It was only when the coach framed this as "your caring is so powerful that we need to explore how to channel it most effectively" that Supra could begin to examine the unintended consequences of her empathy without feeling attacked.

The Art of Compassionate Confrontation Helping clients see their shadows requires what I call "compassionate confrontation" the ability to surface difficult truths in ways that increase rather than decrease the client's capacity to hear and act on them. This involves:

Leading with Strength Recognition: Always acknowledging the positive intention and genuine capability before exploring shadows.

Using Data and Observation: Focusing on specific behaviors and outcomes rather than character judgments.

Exploring Impact vs. Intent: Helping clients understand that good intentions don't always translate to positive impact.

Inviting Curiosity: Framing shadow exploration as interesting puzzles to solve rather than problems to fix.

A skilled coach might say: "I see how much you care about getting things right. Your attention to detail has clearly contributed to your success. I'm curious about what happens when that attention to detail meets tight deadlines. Could we explore some specific situations where this dynamic has played out?"

The Coach as Guide: Navigating the Development Journey

Developmental Sequencing Strengths-shadow work must be carefully sequenced to match the client's developmental readiness. Pushing too hard too fast, can create resistance or overwhelm; moving too slowly can leave clients stuck in ineffective patterns.

The general sequence typically involves:

1. ***Strengths Appreciation***: Ensuring the client has a solid foundation of strengths awareness and appreciation.
2. ***Shadow Recognition***: Gently introducing the concept that strengths can be overused
3. ***Pattern Identification***: Helping the client recognize their specific overuse patterns
4. ***Impact Exploration***: Examining the consequences of overuse on self and others
5. ***Experimentation***: Trying new approaches and calibrations
6. ***Integration***: Developing consistent practices for conscious strength use

Matching Interventions to Learning Styles

Different people learn about their strengths and shadows in different ways. Effective coaches adapt their approach to match the client's learning preferences:

Analytical Learners: Provide frameworks, assessments, and data-driven insights *Experiential Learners*: Create opportunities for real-time practice and immediate feedback *Reflective Learners*: Use journaling, meditation, and deep conversation *Social Learners*: Incorporate peer feedback, group coaching, and team exercises

The Coach as Catalyst: Facilitating Experiments and Growth

Designing Developmental Experiments One of the most powerful tools in strengths-shadow work is the developmental experiment a carefully designed opportunity for the client to try new approaches and observe the results. Effective experiments are:

Specific: Focus on particular behaviors in defined contexts

Safe: Low-risk opportunities where failure won't have serious consequences

Observable: Include clear ways to measure results and gather feedback

Reflective: Built-in time for processing learning and insights

For Marcus, the relationship-building sales leader, his coach designed an experiment where he would practice being more direct and challenging in client conversations. They identified specific low-risk situations where he could try this approach and established criteria for evaluating the results.

Building Feedback Systems Since one of the biggest challenges in strengths development is getting accurate information about how our strengths are being received, coaches play a crucial role in helping clients build better feedback systems. This might involve:

- Teaching clients how to ask for useful feedback
- Helping them identify trusted advisors who can provide honest input
- Creating structured opportunities for peer feedback
- Developing self-monitoring practices that increase awareness

Supporting Integration Over Time. Real behavior change takes time, and the integration of strengths-shadow awareness into daily practice is an ongoing process. Coaches support this integration by:

Regular Check-ins: Scheduled conversations to review progress and challenges *Accountability Structures*: Systems for tracking commitments and celebrating progress. *Obstacle Problem-Solving*: Helping clients navigate setbacks and resistance *Success Amplification*: Identifying and building on what's working well

Advanced Coaching Interventions

The Brilliance-Blindspot Navigator One powerful tool involves creating a visual map of the client's strengths and their corresponding shadows, including:

- Specific behaviors associated with each
- Contexts where each is most likely to emerge
- Early warning signs of overuse
- Strategies for catching and correcting overuse

The Brilliance-Blindspot Navigator

A Worksheet for Conscious Strength Development

Name: ______________________

Date: ______________________

Instructions:

a. Identify your top 3–5 signature strengths using the sections below.

b. For each strength, complete all sections thoughtfully and honestly.

c. Use specific examples and situations from your experience.

d. Review and update this worksheet quarterly for ongoing development.

e. Share insights with a coach, mentor, or trusted colleague for additional perspective.

- STRENGTH #1: ______________________________
    - *(e.g., Strategic Thinking, Empathy, Leadership)*
- **Brilliance Zone**
  When does this strength serve you exceptionally well?
  Consider contexts, behaviors, and outcomes.
  Write about your peak performance moments with this strength...

- **Blindspot Zone**
  When does this strength become problematic or counterproductive? What are the overuse behaviors?
  Describe situations where this strength has backfired...
- **Trigger Alert System**
  What situations, emotions, or conditions typically trigger the overuse of this strength?
  List your specific triggers (stress, deadlines, difficult people, high-stakes situations, etc.) ...
- **Early Warning Signals**
  How do you know when you're moving from brilliance into blind spot territory?
  What are your internal and external cues?
  Describe the warning signs you can watch for (thoughts, feelings, others' reactions, energy levels, etc.) ...
- **Recalibration Toolkit**
  What specific strategies will you use to return to optimal strength usage when you notice overuse?
  List your concrete action steps (pause techniques, reframing strategies, alternative approaches, etc.)...

- STRENGTH #2: ________________________________

  (e.g., Strategic Thinking, Empathy, Leadership)

- **Brilliance Zone**
  When does this strength serve you exceptionally well?
  Consider contexts, behaviors, and outcomes.
  Write about your peak performance moments with this strength...
- **Blindspot Zone**
  When does this strength become problematic or counterproductive?
  What are the overuse behaviors?
  Describe situations where this strength has backfired...
- **Trigger Alert System**
  What situations, emotions, or conditions typically trigger the

overuse of this strength?
List your specific triggers (stress, deadlines, difficult people, high-stakes situations, etc.)...

- **Early Warning Signals**
  How do you know when you're moving from brilliance into blind spot territory?
  What are your internal and external cues?
  Describe the warning signs you can watch for (thoughts, feelings, others' reactions, energy levels, etc.) ...
- **Recalibration Toolkit**
  What specific strategies will you use to return to optimal strength usage when you notice overuse?
  List your concrete action steps (pause techniques, reframing strategies, alternative approaches, etc.)...

- STRENGTH #3: ________________________________
  - (e.g., Strategic Thinking, Empathy, Leadership)
- **Brilliance Zone**
  When does this strength serve you exceptionally well? Consider contexts, behaviors, and outcomes.
  Write about your peak performance moments with this strength...
- **Blindspot Zone**
  When does this strength become problematic or counterproductive? What are the overuse behaviors?
  Describe situations where this strength has backfired...
- **Trigger Alert System**
  What situations, emotions, or conditions typically trigger the overuse of this strength?
- List your specific triggers (stress, deadlines, difficult people, high-stakes situations, etc.)...
- **Early Warning Signals**
  How do you know when you're moving from brilliance into blind spot territory?
  What are your internal and external cues?

Describe the warning signs you can watch for (thoughts, feelings, others' reactions, energy levels, etc.) ...

- **Recalibration Toolkit**
  What specific strategies will you use to return to optimal strength usage when you notice overuse?
  List your concrete action steps (pause techniques, reframing strategies, alternative approaches, etc.) ...

Reflection & Integration

1. What patterns do you notice across your strengths and their shadows?

____

2. Which strength shadow is most problematic for you currently?

____

3. What support or accountability do you need to develop better strength calibration?

____

4. What's one specific commitment you'll make based on these insights?

____

Note: For optimal development, complete this assessment quarterly and share insights with a coach or mentor.

The Inner Board of Directors This exercise helps clients personify different aspects of their personality, including their various strengths and shadows. By giving voice to these different "parts," clients can better understand internal conflicts and make more conscious choices about which aspects to activate in different situations.

The Opposite Day Challenge For clients who are heavily identified with particular strengths, experimenting with their "opposite" can be revelatory. The analytical thinker spends a day making only intuitive decisions; the collaborative leader practices being directive; the optimist allows themselves to be realistic about problems.

Organizational Applications: Creating Cultures of Conscious Strength Use

The Organizational Shadow

Just as individuals can overuse their strengths, organizations can develop collective shadows around their most valued capabilities. A company that prides itself on innovation might become so focused on the next new thing that it fails to execute well on existing products. An organization known for its analytical rigor might become paralyzed by analysis when quick decisions are needed.

Understanding organizational shadows requires examining:

- What strengths does the organization most celebrate and reward?
- What capabilities are seen as less valuable or are actively discouraged?
- How do the organization's strengths show up under pressure or stress?
- What feedback does the organization get from customers, partners, or other stakeholders about potential overuse?

Case Study:

The Innovation Trap Tech Global was a software company renowned for its innovative products and creative culture. The organization attracted brilliant engineers and designers who thrived on solving complex problems and creating breakthrough solutions. However, as the company grew, its innovation strength began to create shadows:

- Products became increasingly complex, making them harder to use and support
- Teams would abandon projects before completion when more interesting challenges emerged
- The company struggled to maintain and improve existing products, always chasing the next big thing
- Customers began complaining about reliability and consistency issues

The company's innovation strength was still valuable, but it needed to be balanced with complementary capabilities like execution excellence, customer focus, and operational discipline.

Building Strengths-Aware Leadership

Developing Leaders Who Can Navigate Complexity. Organizations need leaders who can model conscious strength use and help others develop this capability. This requires:

Self-Aware Leaders: Who understand their own strength patterns and shadows *Contextually Intelligent Leaders*: Who can read situations and adjust their approach accordingly. *Developmentally Minded Leaders*: Who see helping others develop strengths intelligence as a key leadership responsibility.

Leadership Development Programs. Effective leadership development programs increasingly incorporate strengths-shadow work through:

- 360-degree feedback focused on strength overuse patterns
- Action learning projects that require leaders to stretch beyond their comfort zones
- Peer coaching relationships that provide ongoing feedback and support
- Mentoring programs that pair leaders with different strength profiles

Team Dynamics and Strengths Balance

Creating Complementary Teams While it's tempting to create teams of people with similar strengths (since they often work well together initially), the most effective teams typically have complementary strength profiles. This requires:

Intentional Team Composition: Considering strengths balance when forming teams *Clear Role Definition*: Helping team members understand how their unique strengths contribute to team success *Conflict Navigation*: Teaching teams how to work through the tensions that naturally arise when different strengths interact *Shared Language*: Developing common vocabulary for discussing strengths and shadows

The Team Shadow Map Just as individuals can map their strengths and shadows, teams can create collective maps that show:

- The team's dominant strengths and potential blind spots
- How individual shadows might be amplified or mitigated by team dynamics
- Situations where the team's strength profile is likely to be most and least effective
- Strategies for accessing less dominant but necessary capabilities

Organizational Systems and Processes

Performance Management Traditional performance management systems often focus heavily on fixing weaknesses rather than managing strengths effectively. A strengths-shadow approach to performance management includes:

- Regular conversations about how strengths are being applied and their effectiveness
- Development goals that focus on strengths calibration rather than just strengths building
- Recognition systems that value not just strength use but contextually appropriate strength use
- Career pathing that considers strengths fit and development opportunities

Hiring and Selection Organizations can improve their hiring processes by:

- Assessing not just whether candidates have certain strengths, but whether they can apply them contextually
- Looking for evidence of self-awareness and ability to adapt strength application
- Considering how candidates' strength profiles will complement existing team dynamics

- Asking behavioral questions that reveal both strengths and awareness of their shadows

Culture and Values Organizations can reinforce conscious strength use through:

- Values statements that emphasize balance and contextual awareness
- Stories and examples that celebrate not just strength use but wise strength use
- Communication that normalizes discussion of shadows and overuse
- Policies and procedures that build in checks against strength overuse

Advanced Applications: Strengths-Shadow Work in Complex Contexts

Cross-Cultural Considerations

The expression and perception of strengths vary significantly across cultures, making strengths-shadow work particularly complex in global organizations. What's considered confident leadership in one culture might be seen as arrogant disrespect in another. What's viewed as collaborative decision-making in one context might be perceived as indecisive weakness in another.

Cultural Intelligence and Strengths Calibration Working effectively across cultures requires developing cultural intelligence around strengths:

- Understanding how your natural strengths are likely to be perceived in different cultural contexts
- Develop the ability to recognize cultural cues that suggest your strengths might need to be amplified or moderated. Developing sensitivity to how others' cultural backgrounds might influence their strength expression

- Building skills for navigating cultural tensions around different approaches to strength use

Case Study:

The Global Team Challenge Maria led a global product development team with members from the United States, Germany, Japan, and Brazil. Her natural collaborative style worked well with some team members but created challenges with others:

- Her German colleagues appreciated her thoroughness but sometimes found her consensus-building approach inefficient
- Her Japanese team members valued her inclusive style but were uncomfortable with direct confrontation when conflicts arose
- Her Brazilian colleagues enjoyed her relationship focus but sometimes needed more decisive direction
- Her American colleagues liked her openness to input but occasionally wanted faster decision-making

Through strengths-shadow coaching, Maria learned to calibrate her collaborative strength differently with different team members while maintaining her authentic leadership style.

Crisis Leadership and Strength Adaptation

Crisis situations often require leaders to adapt their strengths dramatically. The participative leader might need to become more directive; the analytical thinker might need to make decisions with incomplete information; the relationship-focused leader might need to make unpopular decisions quickly.

The Crisis Strengths Framework During crises, leaders need to consider:

Speed vs. Thoroughness: How to balance the need for quick action with the need for quality decisions *Individual vs. Collective Needs*: When to prioritize organizational survival over individual preferences or needs *Communication Intensity*: How to increase communication frequency and directness without overwhelming people *Strength Flexibility*: Which strengths to dial up, dial down, or temporarily set aside

Building Crisis Adaptability Organizations can help leaders develop crisis adaptability through:

- Scenario planning exercises that require different strength applications
- Crisis simulations that provide safe opportunities to practice strength flexibility
- After-action reviews that examine how strengths were applied during actual crises
- Cross-training that exposes leaders to different strength approaches

Strengths-Shadow Work in High-Stakes Environments

Some environments such as emergency medicine, military operations, or financial trading require extremely refined strengths calibration because the consequences of overuse can be severe.

Precision Calibration In high-stakes environments, strengths calibration must be extremely precise:

- *Hypervigilance Training*: Developing acute awareness of internal states and external cues
- *Rapid Recovery Skills*: Learning to quickly recognize and correct strength overuse
- *Team Backup Systems*: Creating redundant systems where others can compensate for individual overuse
- *Stress Inoculation*: Practicing strength calibration under artificially stressful conditions

CHAPTER 19
The 7 Spiral Coaching Steps Model for Effective Leadership

Effective leadership requires more than just giving directions; it demands the ability to coach others towards their goals. Dr. Valeria Lo Iacono's 7 **Spiral Coaching Steps Model** provides leaders with a structured yet flexible approach to coaching that recognizes learning and development as non-linear processes. This chapter explores how leaders can use this powerful model to become more effective coaches and, consequently, more successful managers.

Why This Model Transforms Leadership Practice

Throughout my years of working with leaders and coaching professionals, I have consistently observed a fundamental gap between what leaders know they should do and what they actually practice in their daily interactions with team members. Most leaders understand the importance of developing their people, yet when faced with pressing deadlines and immediate challenges, they default to directive leadership, simply telling people what to do rather than coaching them through the thinking process. While this approach may seem efficient in the short term, it creates a dangerous dependency cycle where employees become increasingly reliant on their leader's decisions, ultimately limiting both individual growth and organizational capability. Dr. Lo Iacono's 7 Spiral Coaching Steps Model addresses this challenge by providing a practical framework that leaders can use even in time-pressured situations, transforming everyday interactions into developmental opportunities without sacrificing productivity or results.

What particularly drew me to include this model in our coaching toolkit is its revolutionary spiral concept, which acknowledges a truth that many traditional coaching approaches ignore: human development is messy, non-linear, and often requires revisiting earlier stages of the process. In my experience working with diverse teams across various industries like aviation and IT, I have witnessed countless coaching initiatives fail because they were built on the assumption that people learn in straight lines, that once they understand their goal, assess their situation, and create an action plan, they simply execute it without deviation. The reality is far different. People encounter unexpected obstacles, gain new insights that change their perspective, discover resources they didn't know they had, or realize their original goals weren't quite right. Traditional linear coaching models often leave both coaches and clients feeling frustrated when they need to "go backward" in the process. Dr. Lo Iacono's spiral approach normalizes this natural learning pattern, making it a strength rather than a weakness. This model gives leaders permission to be flexible and adaptive in their coaching while still maintaining structure and momentum toward desired outcomes. The spiral design also reflects how real organizational change happens rarely in neat, predictable stages, but rather through iterative cycles of experimentation, learning, and adjustment that ultimately create sustainable transformation.

Understanding the Spiral Coaching Steps Model

The most distinctive and revolutionary feature of Dr. Lo Iacono's model lies in its spiral structure, which fundamentally challenges the conventional wisdom of linear coaching approaches. Traditional coaching models assume that development follows a predictable sequence where individuals move from one stage to the next in a neat, orderly progression. However, Dr. Lo Iacono recognized that this linear thinking fails to capture the messy, complex reality of how people actually learn, grow, and solve problems. Her spiral model acknowledges that progress in coaching is rarely straightforward and that the seven steps Outcome, Situation, Options, Goals, Steps, Action, and Review form an interconnected spiral because coaches and clients inevitably need to revisit earlier stages as new insights emerge, circumstances change, or deeper understanding develops.

This spiral approach reflects the authentic reality of human development and problem-solving processes. In real-world coaching situations, people don't simply identify an outcome and march steadily toward it. Instead, as they gain new perspectives, encounter unexpected challenges, receive feedback, or discover hidden assumptions, they naturally need to reconsider their original outcomes, reassess their situation with fresh eyes, or explore different options that weren't initially apparent. Rather than viewing this as regression or failure, the spiral model celebrates these iterations as essential elements of deep learning and sustainable change. The model's inherent flexibility makes it particularly valuable for leaders who need to adapt their coaching style to different situations, personalities, and organizational contexts while maintaining a coherent framework for development.

The Seven Spiral Coaching Steps - A Comprehensive Framework

Step 1: Outcome - Setting the Visionary Foundation

The first step in Dr. Lo Iacono's model focuses on helping clients identify and articulate their desired outcome, but this goes far beyond simply stating what they want to achieve. This step is fundamentally about creating an inspiring, energizing vision that serves as the North Star for the entire coaching journey. Unlike goal-setting, which comes later in the process, outcome identification is about painting a picture of success that is both ambitious and personally meaningful. The outcome stage encourages clients to think expansively about possibilities without being immediately constrained by current limitations or perceived barriers.

The power of this step lies in its ability to tap into what truly motivates the client at a deep level. When people connect with an outcome that genuinely excites them, they develop intrinsic motivation that sustains them through challenges and setbacks. Dr. Lo Iacono's approach emphasizes three critical principles that make outcomes truly powerful. First, the "Aim High" principle encourages client to envision their ideal situation without immediately worrying about practical limitations. Like a mountain climber who first sets their sights on the highest peak visible, starting with an ambitious vision allows for intelligent scaling back later, if necessary, but prevents the self-limiting thinking that occurs when people start with realistic expectations.

The second principle, positive framing, recognizes that how we articulate outcomes significantly impacts our emotional connection to them. Outcomes framed in terms of what we want to create, achieve, or become are inherently more inspiring than those focused on avoiding problems or preventing negative situations. For example, "creating an indestructible product" generates more energy and creativity than "making a product that doesn't break after first use." This positive framing activates different neural pathways and promotes solution-focused thinking rather than problem-focused rumination.

The third and perhaps most crucial principle is ownership. The client must genuinely own their outcome for the coaching process to be effective. While leaders may be tempted to impose their vision or redirect clients toward outcomes that align with organizational priorities, this approach typically backfires by undermining intrinsic motivation and reducing commitment. When people feel that they're working toward someone else's vision, their engagement naturally diminishes, and they're more likely to abandon the effort when faced with obstacles.

Practical application of this step involves asking powerful questions that help clients connect with their deepest aspirations. Questions like "In an ideal world, what would success look like?" or "If resources were unlimited, what would you achieve?" help people move beyond their current constraints and tap into their authentic desires. The coach's role is to listen deeply, ask clarifying questions, and help the client articulate their vision in compelling, personal terms. If a client's initial vision seems limited or lacks energy, the skilled coach explores what might be holding them back rather than imposing a more ambitious alternative.

Step 2: Situation - Conducting Objective Reality Assessment

The second step involves helping clients develop a clear, objective understanding of their current situation, which serves as the crucial starting point for any meaningful change effort. This step is deceptively complex because it requires moving beyond surface-level descriptions to develop a deep, nuanced understanding of the present reality. The situation assessment must be comprehensive enough to inform intelligent decision-making while remaining focused on factors that are genuinely relevant to achieving the desired outcome.

This step explores multiple dimensions of the current situation, including available resources, existing capabilities, environmental factors, and recent developments that might impact the coaching journey. The assessment examines not just what resources the client currently has, but also what resources they need to achieve their outcome. It identifies strengths they can leverage and weaknesses they need to address or work around. Importantly, it establishes their current position relative to their desired outcome, creating a clear sense of the gap that needs to be bridged.

Maintaining objectivity during this assessment is critical but challenging. Human beings naturally filter information through their emotions, assumptions, and past experiences, which can distort their perception of reality. Effective coaches help clients move beyond subjective interpretations to develop fact-based understanding. This involves encouraging detailed descriptions rather than evaluative judgments, asking for specific observations about what they saw, heard, and experienced, and using neutral language that avoids emotionally loaded implications.

The questioning approach in this step requires particular skill. "Why" questions, while seemingly logical, often trigger defensive responses because they can feel like challenges to the client's judgment or competence. More effective alternatives include "What was your thought process?" or "What factors influenced your decision?" which gather the same information while maintaining a collaborative, non-threatening tone. The goal is to create a comprehensive, accurate picture of the current situation that serves as a solid foundation for subsequent steps in the coaching process.

Example questions that prove particularly effective include "What resources do you currently have available?" which inventories existing assets; "What specific strengths can you draw upon?" which identifies capabilities that can be leveraged; "Where exactly are you now in relation to your desired outcome?" which quantifies the gap; and "What has happened so far that's relevant to this situation?" which captures important historical context and recent developments.

Step 3: Options - Unleashing Creative Possibility Thinking

The third step represents one of the most energizing and creative phases of the coaching process, focusing on generating as many potential solutions, approaches, and pathways as possible. This step operates on the principle that the quality of available options directly influences the quality of eventual outcomes, making broad exploration essential before narrowing down to specific choices. The emphasis here is deliberately on quantity over immediate quality evaluation and refinement comes later in the process.

One of the greatest challenges in this step involves helping clients overcome the mental barriers and limiting assumptions that constrain their thinking. These barriers often manifest as automatic thoughts that shut down creative exploration before it can fully develop. Common limiting assumptions include "This can't be done," "It's never been tried before," "It's too expensive," "They'll never agree," or "We don't have time." While these concerns may ultimately prove valid, introducing them too early in the options generation process severely limits creative thinking and prevents the discovery of innovative solutions.

Effective coaches employ various techniques to expand the client's thinking beyond these natural constraints. Hypothetical questions like "What if money were unlimited?" or "What if time weren't a factor?" temporarily remove common barriers and allow for more expansive thinking. Role modeling questions such as "What would someone you admire do in this situation?" or "What would a superhero do?" tap into different perspectives and can reveal approaches that wouldn't occur under normal circumstances.

Creating a judgment-free environment is essential for this step to be effective. Clients must feel completely safe to express wild, impractical, or seemingly silly ideas without fear of criticism or ridicule. Often, the most innovative solutions emerge from ideas that initially seem absurd but contain kernels of insight that can be developed into viable approaches. The coach's role is to encourage continued brainstorming, celebrate creative thinking, and resist the urge to evaluate or critique options as they emerge.

The visual presentation of options also matters more than many coaches realize. Mapping options side by side rather than creating a numbered list helps avoid the implication of hierarchy or priority, which can subtly influence the client's thinking. The goal is to maintain equal consideration for all possibilities until the evaluation phase begins.

When coaches have ideas, they'd like to contribute, timing and approach are crucial. The most effective practice involves waiting until clients have exhausted their own options before offering input. Even then, asking permission "I have an idea. Would you like to hear it? "Maintains the collaborative relationship and respects the client's ownership of the process. This approach allows coaches to contribute their expertise while preserving the client's sense of agency and creative ownership.

Step 4: Goals - Transforming Vision into Concrete Direction

The fourth step represents a crucial transition point where abstract ideas and possibilities transform into concrete, actionable goals that provide clear direction for subsequent action. This step bridges the gap between the expansive thinking of the options phase and the practical planning that follows. After clients have evaluated their various options and selected the most promising approaches, they must craft specific goals that translate their chosen direction into measurable, achievable targets.

The SMART goal framework provides essential structure for this transformation, ensuring that goals possess the characteristics necessary for effective implementation. Specific goals eliminate ambiguity and provide clear direction for action. Rather than vague aspirations like "improve communication," specific goals define exactly what improvement looks like: "conduct weekly team meetings with a structured agenda and follow-up action items." Measurable goals establish clear success criteria that enable progress tracking and completion recognition. Without measurable elements, it becomes impossible to determine whether goals have been achieved or how much progress has been made.

Achievable goals strike the crucial balance between ambition and realism. While goals should stretch the client's capabilities and inspire growth, they must remain within the realm of possibility given available resources, constraints, and time frames. Goals that are too easy fail to motivate, while those that are impossibly difficult lead to frustration and abandonment. The coach's role involves helping clients calibrate their goals to find this optimal challenge level.

Relevant goals maintain a clear connection to the client's original outcome and hold genuine meaning for them personally. Goals that feel imposed or disconnected from the client's intrinsic motivations struggle to sustain effort over time. The relevance criterion ensures that goal achievement contributes meaningfully to the larger vision that initiated the coaching process.

Time-bound goals establish clear deadlines and create urgency that drives action. Without time constraints, goals tend to drift indefinitely as other priorities compete for attention. Effective deadlines are specific rather than vague, creating accountability and enabling progress measurement.

The goal-setting strategy often involves starting with one overarching goal that captures the essential direction, then breaking it down into smaller, more manageable sub-goals if the original proves too complex or overwhelming. This hierarchical approach helps maintain motivation by providing regular opportunities for achievement and progress recognition. Each sub-goal completion creates momentum and builds confidence for tackling subsequent challenges.

Step 5: Steps - Crafting Detailed Implementation Roadmaps

The fifth step transforms well-defined goals into detailed, actionable implementation plans that specify exactly what needs to be done, when, and by whom. This step represents the bridge between strategic thinking and tactical execution, converting goals from conceptual targets into practical roadmaps that guide daily actions and decisions. The quality of planning in this step often determines the success or failure of the entire coaching initiative.

Effective action planning addresses multiple dimensions simultaneously. It identifies specific tasks that must be completed, but goes beyond simple task listing to consider the logical sequence of activities, dependencies between different tasks, resource requirements for each step, and realistic timeframes for completion. This comprehensive approach helps prevent common implementation failures that occur when planning is too superficial or optimistic.

Timeline development requires particular attention to detail and realism. Clients often underestimate the time required for complex tasks or fail to account for competing priorities and unexpected obstacles. Skilled coaches help coaching clients think through their schedules realistically, considering not just the time required for focused work on each task, but also the coordination time, review cycles, approval processes, and buffer time for unforeseen complications.

Resource requirement analysis ensures that coaching clients have identified and secured everything they need for successful implementation. Resources include not just financial assets, but also human resources, information, tools, technology, and access to key stakeholders. Failing to identify resource needs early often leads to frustrating delays and stalled progress later in the implementation process.

Dependency mapping reveals the connections between different tasks and identifies critical path activities that must be completed before others can begin. This analysis helps optimize the sequence of activities and prevents bottlenecks that could derail the entire plan. Understanding dependencies also enables more effective risk management by highlighting points where delays in one area could cascade through the entire project.

Perhaps most importantly, this step involves identifying milestones for celebration throughout the implementation process. The power of celebrating small wins cannot be overstated, each completed step represents genuine progress toward the larger goal, and acknowledging these achievements maintains motivation and momentum during challenging periods. Celebrations don't need to be elaborate; often, simple acknowledgment and recognition of progress prove sufficient to sustain energy and commitment.

Step 6: Action - Orchestrating Implementation with Support

The sixth step represents the critical transition from planning to execution, where carefully developed strategies meet the reality of daily life and organizational dynamics. This is often where coaching initiatives succeed or fail, making the coach's role during this phase absolutely crucial. The focus shifts from helping client think through their approach to supporting them as they navigate the inevitable challenges, obstacles, and unexpected developments that arise during implementation.

The coaching leader's responsibilities during this phase are multifaceted and demanding. First and foremost, they must ensure accountability without micromanaging a delicate balance that requires skill and judgment. Accountability involves asking specific, concrete questions that help clients clarify their commitments and create personal responsibility for follow-through. Questions like "What exactly are you going to do?" ensure precision and eliminate ambiguity that could lead to inaction or misdirected effort. "When will you start?" and "When will this be completed?" establish clear timeframes and create urgency. "Who needs to be informed of your plans?" ensures appropriate communication and stakeholder engagement. "How will I know when this is done?" establishes clear completion criteria and reporting mechanisms.

However, accountability without support creates pressure that often leads to stress and eventual breakdown. The second critical responsibility involves offering genuine, practical support throughout the implementation process. This means actively asking what support clients need and then following through to ensure they receive it. Support might involve removing organizational obstacles, providing additional resources, connecting clients with subject matter experts, or simply serving as a sounding board when challenges arise.

The third responsibility involves establishing regular feedback and check-in processes that maintain connection without becoming intrusive. This requires careful calibration- too little contact leaves clients feeling abandoned and struggling with challenges alone, while too much contact feels like micromanagement and undermines their sense of autonomy. Effective feedback planning involves collaborative agreement on meeting frequency, communication methods, and agenda focus that serves the client's ' needs rather than the coach's anxiety about progress.

The fourth and perhaps most underestimated responsibility involves maintaining genuine enthusiasm and encouragement throughout the implementation process. The coach's energy level and emotional support significantly impact the client's motivation and persistence, especially when they encounter setbacks or obstacles. This doesn't mean false cheerfulness or ignoring real problems, but rather maintaining confident optimism about the client's ability to overcome challenges and achieve their goals.

Step 7: Review - Enabling Continuous Learning and Adaptation

The seventh step embodies the heart of the spiral model's philosophy by creating structured opportunities for reflection, learning, and course correction that can lead back to any previous step in the process. This step acknowledges that implementation rarely proceeds exactly according to plan and that the ability to learn from experience and adapt accordingly often distinguishes successful initiatives from failed ones. The review process serves multiple functions simultaneously: monitoring progress, capturing learning, identifying needed adjustments, and maintaining motivation through recognition of achievements.

Review activities must be comprehensive enough to generate genuine insights while remaining practical and manageable within busy schedules. Progress monitoring involves comparing actual results against planned goals and timelines, but goes beyond simple success-or-failure assessment to understand the factors that contributed to outcomes. This deeper analysis helps identify what's working well and should be continued or expanded, as well as what isn't working and needs modification or abandonment.

Reflection on obstacles and opportunities requires particular attention because these often provide the most valuable learning. Obstacles that weren't anticipated during planning reveal gaps in situational assessment or option generation that can inform future coaching initiatives. Similarly, unexpected opportunities that emerge during implementation might suggest modifications to goals or approaches that could lead to even better outcomes than originally envisioned.

The adjustment process that follows review can involve changes at any level of the spiral model. Sometimes, clients discover that their original situation assessment was incomplete or inaccurate, requiring a return to Step 2 for deeper analysis. Other times, implementation experience reveals new options that weren't considered initially, suggesting a return to Step 3 for expanded possibility thinking. Goals might need modification based on what's learned during implementation, or action steps might require revision based on practical experience.

The spiral nature of this model becomes most apparent during the review phase, Dr. Lo Iacono's model highlights the dynamic nature of the process, indicating possible returns to earlier stages. This isn't viewed as failure or regression, but rather as natural evolution and learning. Based on their implementation experiences, client's might need to reassess their situation with new information, consider options that weren't initially apparent, modify goals based on changed circumstances, adjust action steps based on practical constraints, or even reconsider their original outcome based on deeper self-understanding.

This flexibility represents the model's greatest strength it acknowledges that learning and development are inherently iterative processes that require multiple cycles of action and reflection to achieve optimal results. Rather than forcing artificial linearity onto naturally spiral processes, Dr. Lo Iacono's model works with human psychology and organizational reality to create sustainable change and continuous improvement.

Coaching Implementation

The client is **Elena**, a sales manager for Spain and Italy. She is being coached by her team leader to take on responsibility for the German market expansion.

1. Outcome – What do you want to achieve?

Coach: "Elena, let's start with your bigger picture. What would success look like for you in your new role handling the German market?"

Elena: "I'd like to establish our organic coffee presence in Germany ideally becoming one of the top three in that market segment."

Coach (guidance): Helps her refine this into a **personal vision** aligned with the team's vision:

"My outcome is to successfully lead the entry of our organic coffee into the German market by building brand awareness and customer trust."

2. Situation – Where are you now?

Coach: "Can you walk me through where things stand right now with your efforts in Germany?"

Elena:

- No German-language web presence.
- Limited brand recognition in Germany.
- Strong presence in Spain/Italy but unfamiliar with German consumer behavior.
- A recent competitor just launched a German website.

Coach (reflection prompt): "What's working from your past markets that might not work in Germany? What feels like a barrier right now?"

3. Options – What could you do?

Coach: "Let's explore some possibilities. What strategies can you think of to build our brand in Germany?"

Elena brainstorms ideas:

- Launch a German-language website
- Partner with eco-friendly influencers in Germany
- Offer samples through German organic stores
- Attend local food and wellness expos

Coach (deepening): "What are the pros and cons of each? What would be easiest to implement first, and what might have the most impact?"

4. Goals – What will you do?

Coach: "Let's narrow it down. What's your priority goal over the next few months?"

Elena (with guidance): "Create a 50-page German-language website about our organic coffee range by the end of the fiscal year."

Coach: "Let's make that SMART – Specific, Measurable, Achievable, Relevant, and Time-bound."

They refine the goal:

Goal: "By March 31st, I will launch a 50-page German-language website featuring our organic coffee line, including translated product pages, blog posts, and an about-us section."

5. Steps – How will you get there?

Coach: "What would the milestones look like between now and then?"

Elena outlines tasks with support:

- Week 1–2: Hire a bilingual web designer
- Week 3–6: Develop and translate content
- Week 7–10: Upload content, run SEO checks
- Week 11–12: Internal testing and soft launch
- Week 13: Full launch and promotion campaign

Coach (tracking): "Who else do you need on board for this? What might cause delays?"

6. Action – Who does what and when?

Coach: "Let's assign responsibilities and set some check-in points."

Elena:

- Owns content creation and translation oversight
- Delegates design to agency
- Schedules bi-weekly progress updates with her coach

Coach: "Let's schedule our next 1:1 to review progress and adjust anything if needed."

7. Review – What have you learned? What's next?

Two weeks later...

Elena (update): "We hired a designer, but we found out our competitor launched a very similar site. Their SEO is quite aggressive."

Coach: "Interesting. That changes the landscape a bit. Let's go back to Step 3 – Options – and rethink how you might differentiate."

They revisit ideas like:

- Creating interactive product comparison tools
- Adding customer testimonials in German
- Incorporating sustainability metrics visibly on each page

Coach (meta-reflection): "What has this process taught you about leading in new markets? How can you use this learning going forward?"

Using the 7 Spiral Coaching Steps Model in this one-on-one context allowed me to support Elena in a structured yet flexible way, helping her navigate uncertainty, clarify her goals, and take purposeful action. The model's spiral nature proved especially valuable when circumstances changed, enabling us to revisit and adapt earlier steps without losing momentum. Whether used in formal coaching sessions or informal conversations, this approach fosters ownership, reflection, and resilience, empowering individuals to grow as proactive, confident leaders in dynamic environments.

The End Is the Beginning

Every transformative journey brings you to a sacred threshold that breathtaking moment when you realize what felt like an ending was actually your most powerful beginning.

As you turn to these final pages, I'm not offering you closure. I'm extending an invitation to step boldly into the fullness of who you've become: a coach. Every moment of reflection, every breakthrough, every quiet inner shift you've experienced wasn't just preparation it was your awakening. Now it's time to take that fire within you and illuminate the world through your calling.

In these closing chapters, we're turning our attention outward to the tangible, soul-aligned building blocks of your coaching career. This is where your personal metamorphosis meets your professional destiny.

Here's the journey that awaits you:

Discovering Your Unique Coaching Signature

You weren't meant to be just another coach. In an arena rich with possibilities from transformational life coaching to executive presence, from wellness architecture to healing trauma your authentic specialization becomes your North Star. Together, we'll uncover how your personal story, core values, and natural gifts converge into a niche that doesn't just make sense it makes your soul sing while serving the world's deepest needs.

Mastering Your Craft with Heart and Precision

True coaching transcends good intentions and natural empathy it's a sacred profession that demands your complete excellence. This chapter will guide you in sharpening your skills, embracing ethical mastery, and staying vibrant in an ever-evolving field. Through purposeful certification, meaningful peer partnerships, wise supervision, and deep reflective practice, you'll evolve from a good coach into an extraordinary one.

Building a Coaching Practice That Honors Your Vision

Passion without structure is just a beautiful dream. The other half of your success story is the foundation you build beneath your inspiration. We'll walk through authentic branding, sustainable business models, magnetic client attraction, aligned pricing, protective contracts, authentic visibility, and visionary long-term strategy. Your goal isn't simply to coach it's to flourish as the coach you're meant to be, with unshakeable clarity and quiet confidence.

This isn't your conclusion. This is the moment your spiral opens wide, reaching toward infinite possibility.

Let's begin again this time, as the coach you were always destined to become.

CHAPTER 20

Discovering Your Unique Coaching Signature Through Ikigai

The Ancient Wisdom That Reveals Your Coaching Destiny

High in the serene mountains of Okinawa lies a secret to longevity a way of life practiced by people who've turned living well into an art. Among them exist a profound concept that has guided generations toward purposeful, fulfilling lives. *Ikigai* translates literally as "life's purpose" or "reason for being" but its essence runs far deeper than any simple translation can capture.

Ikigai represents the sacred intersection where four fundamental elements of human fulfillment converge: what you love, what you're naturally gifted at, what the world desperately needs, and what can sustain you financially. It's not merely a career framework it's a philosophy of living that honors both your deepest authenticity and your highest service to others.

For the Okinawans, ikigai isn't something you find once and hold onto forever. It's a living, breathing awareness that evolves as you do, guiding every season of your existence with quiet wisdom. It explains why these remarkable people don't have a word for "retirement" because when you're living your ikigai, why would you ever want to stop?

As coaches, we have the extraordinary privilege of helping others discover their own ikigai. But before we can guide others to this sacred intersection, we must first uncover our own. And here's the beautiful truth: your coaching signature that unique blend of expertise, passion, and service that only you can offer lives precisely at the heart of your ikigai.

Why Specialization Is Your Superpower, Not Your Limitation

In a world saturated with generalist coaches, specialization isn't just recommended it's essential for both your success and your clients' transformation. Yet many emerging coaches resist niching down, fearing they'll limit their opportunities or exclude potential clients. This fear, while understandable, fundamentally misunderstands how true mastery and meaningful impact are created.

The Paradox of Specialization: Going Narrow to Go Deep

When you try to serve everyone, you end up serving no one exceptionally well. Think of it this way: would you rather go to a general practitioner for brain surgery, or seek out a neurosurgeon who has dedicated their entire career to understanding the intricate workings of the brain? The choice is obvious.

The same principle applies to coaching. When you specialize, you don't lose opportunities you create magnetic attraction for the exact people who need your particular genius. You become the obvious choice rather than just another option.

The Neurobiological Reality: How Specialization Creates Expertise

Neuroscience reveals that expertise emerges through focused, deliberate practice in specific domains. When you repeatedly work with similar challenges, patterns, and populations, your brain develops what researchers call "expert pattern recognition." You begin to see solutions that generalists miss, anticipate obstacles before they arise, and guide clients through transformations with an efficiency that feels almost magical.

This isn't just about accumulating hours it's about developing neural pathways that allow you to access deeper insights, more nuanced interventions, and more precise guidance. Your specialized brain becomes a finely tuned instrument capable of creating profound change in your chosen domain.

The Authority Advantage: Why Specialists Command Premium Investment

Clients don't just want coaching they want the right coaching for their specific situation. When someone is struggling with executive presence, they're not looking for a life coach who "also does some leadership work." They're seeking a specialist who breathes executive development, who has guided dozens of leaders through similar challenges, who speaks their language and understands their unique pressures.

Specialists command higher fees not because they're being greedy, but because they deliver exponentially higher value. They can often achieve in months what a generalist might take years to accomplish if they can achieve it at all.

The Marketing Mathematics: Why Niches Multiply the Impact

At first glance, it may seem that casting a wider net brings more opportunities but in reality, influence grows stronger when you focus on a niche. When you specialize, your marketing becomes laser-focused and deeply resonant. You speak directly to your ideal client's real challenges, use language that mirrors their thoughts, and create content that makes them feel truly seen and understood.

A relationship coach who specializes in helping couples navigate the transition to parenthood can create content that stops new parents in their tracks with recognition. In the same way, a business coach who focuses on solo or boutique entrepreneurs can tackle challenges that broader-market coaches often miss entirely.

The Shared Praise Revolution: How Specialists Become Magnetic

When you're known for a specific expertise, people don't talk about "a good coach "they share the story of *the coach who truly listened, understood their struggles, and guided them forward*. These stories spread naturally inspiring trust and connection. Specialization doesn't just make your work visible…it makes it unforgettable.

Your niche becomes your reputation, and your reputation becomes your greatest marketing asset. Other experts start to view you as their torchbearer for specific challenges, generating a steady flow of trusted recommendations.

The Fulfillment Factor: Why Specialization Feeds Your Soul

Perhaps most importantly, specialization allows you to go deep into work that truly matters to you. Instead of surface-level conversations across a broad range of topics, you get to explore the rich complexity of your chosen domain. You become a student of your specialty, continuously deepening your understanding and expanding your toolkit.

This depth creates a virtuous cycle: the more specialized you become, the more fascinated you become by the nuances of your work. Your passion deepens, your expertise grows, and your impact multiplies all while doing work that feels increasingly aligned with your purpose.

The Evolution of Expertise: How Specialization Creates Innovation

When coaches specialize, they don't just serve their niche they advance it. They develop new methodologies, create innovative frameworks, and pioneer approaches that benefit the entire field. The most significant contributions to coaching have come from specialists who went deep enough to see what others missed.

Your specialization becomes a laboratory for innovation, a space where you can develop, refine, and ultimately contribute something genuinely new to the world of human development.

The Four Sacred Circles of Your Coaching Calling

Imagine four luminous circles, each representing a vital aspect of your being, slowly moving toward each other like celestial bodies finding their perfect alignment. Where they intersect that radiant center is where your coaching signature program awaits.

Circle One: What Sets Your Soul Ablaze (Your Passion)

This is the realm of your deepest loves, your most authentic enthusiasms, the topics and experiences that make time disappear. When you're operating in this circle, you feel most alive, most yourself.

Deep Reflection Questions:

- What conversations could you have for hours without ever feeling drained?
- Which human experiences move you to tears both of joy and compassion?
- What injustices in the world stir something fierce and protective within you?
- When do you feel most connected to your own aliveness?
- What aspects of human potential fascinate you endlessly?

Coaching Application: Perhaps you're magnetically drawn to helping women reclaim their voices after years of people-pleasing. Maybe you feel electric when supporting entrepreneurs who are terrified to dream bigger. Or you might discover your passion lies in guiding parents through the beautiful chaos of raising conscious children.

Circle Two: Your Natural Genius (What You Excel At)

These are your innate gifts the abilities that flow through you so naturally that others often marvel at them while you might take them for granted. Your genius isn't just what you've learned; it's what you were born knowing.

Deep Reflection Questions:

- What do people consistently turn to you for help with?
- Which skills feel so natural that you're surprised others find them difficult?
- What patterns do you notice that others seem to miss?
- In what ways do you naturally create transformation in others?
- What compliments do you receive so often that you've started to dismiss them?

Coaching Application: Maybe you have an uncanny ability to help people see their blind spots with compassion rather than judgment. Perhaps you're naturally gifted at helping overwhelmed individuals create systems that actually stick. Or you might possess an intuitive talent for guiding people through major life transitions with grace and wisdom.

Circle Three: The World's Aching Need (What the World Requires)

This circle encompasses the problems that keep you awake at night, the gaps you see that need filling, the healing that you feel called to offer. It's not about what you think should matter it's about what genuinely breaks your heart or stirs your righteous anger.

Deep Reflection Questions:

- What societal problems feel personal to you?

- Which struggles do you see people facing that you know could be transformed?
- What conversations is the world avoiding that desperately need to happen?
- Where do you see people settling for less than they deserve?
- What healing does your community, industry, or generation most need?

Coaching Application: Perhaps you recognize that high-achieving women are burning out at unprecedented rates and need a different model of success. Maybe you see that teenagers are navigating challenges their parents never faced and need specialized support. Or you might notice that spiritual seekers are struggling to integrate their awakening into practical, grounded living.

Circle Four: Your Sustainable Prosperity (What Pays You)

This isn't about chasing money it's about creating sustainable abundance that allows you to serve from a place of overflow rather than depletion. True ikigai recognizes that martyrdom serves no one; you must thrive to give your greatest gifts.

Deep Reflection Questions:

- What would allow you to show up as your most generous, capable self?
- How much financial flow would support your optimal creativity and service?
- What lifestyle supports your deepest values and highest contribution?
- Which markets are actively seeking the transformation you offer?
- How can your gifts create value that people are eager to invest in?

Coaching Application: This might mean recognizing that busy executives will invest significantly in leadership presence coaching because it directly impacts their success. Or discovering that parents will prioritize family harmony coaching because it affects every area of their lives. Perhaps you realize that your gift for trauma-informed coaching serves a growing market of people ready to invest in deep healing.

The Alchemy of Integration: Where Your Circles Converge

The magic doesn't happen in any single circle it emerges in the overlapping spaces, and most powerfully, in the center where all four intersect.

Passion + Excellence = Your Zone of Genius

When what you love meets what you're naturally gifted at, you enter what Gay Hendricks calls your **Zone of Genius** that space where you create extraordinary results with surprising ease.

Excellence + Market Need = Your Professional Competence

Where your gifts meet the world's needs, you find yourself positioned as an expert who can genuinely serve and transform lives.

Market Need + Financial Flow = Your Economic Engine

When the world's needs align with sustainable compensation, you create a viable business model that can grow and thrive.

Financial Flow + Passion = Your Energy Source

When you're compensated well for what you love, you create an energetic cycle that sustains and amplifies your impact.

But the real magic happens in the center where all four circles dance together in perfect harmony.

Crafting Your Signature Program: A Sacred Process

Your ikigai-aligned coaching signature isn't something you create, it's something you uncover. It's been waiting within you, like a seed that needs the right conditions to sprout into full bloom.

Step One: The Deep Dive Discovery

Set aside sacred time ideally a full day or weekend to dive deep into each circle. Use the reflection questions, but don't stop there. Journal, meditate, walk in nature, or engage in whatever practice helps you access your deepest knowing.

Create a visual map with four overlapping circles. As insights arise, place them in the appropriate spaces, noticing what wants to emerge in the overlapping areas.

Step Two: Pattern Recognition

Look for the golden threads that weave through your responses. What themes keep appearing? What energetic signature runs through your various insights? Often, your coaching signature reveals itself as a pattern that's been present throughout your life, waiting for you to recognize its significance.

Step Three: The Integration Exploration

Begin exploring with potential signature programs that honor your ikigai. This might mean:

- Offering pilot sessions to test your hypotheses
- Creating content that explores the intersection of your gifts and the world's needs
- Having conversations with potential clients to understand their deepest challenges and desires
- Prototyping workshops or programs that blend your passion, expertise, market need, and financial sustainability.

Step Four: The Resonance Test

Your true coaching signature will feel like coming home. When you describe it to others, their energy will shift they'll lean in, ask questions, and often say something like, "I've never heard it explained that way before, but that's exactly what I need."

You'll know you've found your ikigai-aligned signature when:

- Exploring it energizes you instead of draining your reserves.
- You feel both excited and slightly nervous (the good kind of nervous that signals growth)

- Potential clients immediately understand the value and transformation you offer
- The work feels sustainable and generative rather than depleting
- You see clear pathways for both impact and income

Living Your Coaching Ikigai

Your ikigai-discovered coaching signature becomes more than a business offering it becomes a way of being in the world. It infuses every client interaction, every piece of content you create, every relationship you build with the authentic essence of who you are and what you're here to contribute.

Remember, ikigai is not a destination but a continuous dance of alignment. As you grow and evolve, so too will your coaching signature. The goal isn't to find the perfect formula and stick to it forever it's to develop the sensitivity and courage to keep returning to this sacred intersection, allowing your work to evolve in harmony with your own becoming.

Your ikigai-aligned coaching signature is your gift to the world and perhaps more importantly, it's your gift to yourself. It's the pathway that allows you to wake up each day knowing that your work is not separate from your purpose, but is the very expression of your deepest reason for being.

In the words of the poet Rainer Maria Rilke: "The purpose of life is to be defeated by greater and greater things." Let your coaching signature be one of those greater things a calling so aligned with your essence that it continuously calls you into the fullest expression of who you're becoming.

The Five Core Competencies: Building Professional Coaching Excellence

Beyond Natural Ability: The Framework for Mastery

There's a fundamental distinction between having natural talent for helping people and possessing the professional competencies that define world-class coaching. While empathy, intuition, and genuine concern provide the foundation, they alone cannot create the consistent, measurable transformations that characterize our profession. True coaching excellence emerges from the systematic development of specific competencies and skills refined through deliberate practice until they become seamlessly integrated into your professional approach.

These competencies serve as the structural framework of coaching mastery. Just as a skilled architect develops precision in design principles and construction techniques, a professional coach cultivates these five core competencies until they flow naturally, creating the optimal environment for client breakthrough and sustainable change.

Competency One: Executive Presence

Executive presence forms the cornerstone upon which all other coaching competencies rest. It's the quality of being completely focused, fully engaged, and strategically aware that your client experiences professional-grade attention and expertise. True presence isn't simply about concentration; it's about creating a field of focused awareness so comprehensive that breakthrough becomes the natural outcome.

Your physical demeanor is your primary professional tool. Clients unconsciously assess your competence through your posture, energy, and self-regulation. When you demonstrate composure and confidence, you create an implicit invitation for your client to access their own clarity and decision-making capacity. Begin each session with intentional breathing and grounding, establishing a confident posture, and maintaining steady eye contact to immediately elevate the professional quality of your engagement.

Expert coaches can remain emotionally engaged without becoming emotionally reactive. When a client shares challenging situations or vulnerable concerns, your ability to stay professionally present, neither rushing to provide solutions nor withdrawing due to discomfort, creates the psychological safety necessary for honest exploration. When you notice the impulse to immediately solve a client's challenge, pause and maintain professional curiosity by asking what perspectives haven't been considered yet.

Mental flexibility involves releasing personal assumptions and maintaining cognitive agility for whatever insights want to emerge. It's the difference between listening to formulate responses and listening to understand completely. When your mind is strategically present, you become a clear mirror reflecting back your client's highest potential and clearest thinking. Set an intention before each session to discover something new about your client's situation, redirecting attention to comprehensive understanding rather than premature solution-making.

Professional presence recognizes that coaching is professional partnership you're engaging with an individual committed to growth and performance improvement. This awareness infuses every interaction with respect and creates space for transformation that extends beyond technique into genuine development.

Common challenges include the consultant's rush to recommendations, which undermines presence by treating client discomfort as an emergency requiring immediate resolution. The expert's assumption eliminates curiosity by believing you understand the situation completely. The performer's pressure blocks authentic engagement by focusing on demonstrating expertise rather than facilitating client success.

Competency Two: Strategic Listening

Strategic listening represents perhaps the most underutilized yet powerful tool in professional coaching. It extends far beyond processing information it's about creating such focused attention that you can identify underlying patterns, systemic issues, and emerging opportunities that your client may not have recognized yet.

Information processing involves listening to the situation, data, and surface narrative. While necessary for context, remaining at this level keeps coaching transactional. You can accurately summarize your client's situation and key details, while recognizing this is only the foundation for deeper work.

Emotional intelligence means attuning to emotional patterns not just what they report feeling, but what you observe in their communication style, pace, and energy. You become fluent in recognizing how emotions impact decision-making and performance. You can identify and reflect emotional patterns that your client hasn't explicitly recognized, helping them develop greater self-awareness and emotional regulation.

Systems thinking in coaching involves recognizing recurring patterns, revealing hidden assumptions, addressing limiting beliefs, and mapping the unseen systems that influence your client's journey. You hear what's not being addressed, what's being avoided, and what patterns are repeating. This is where breakthrough insights typically emerge. You can identify and illuminate systemic patterns that have been outside your client's awareness, creating moments of clarity that shift entire approaches to challenges.

Strategic awareness perceives the client's unrealized potential, their emerging capabilities, and the person they're becoming even when they can't see it themselves. You listen for their strengths and reflect them back until they can leverage them effectively. Your client leaves sessions feeling more connected to their capabilities and potential, regardless of what specific challenges you discussed.

The strategic pause involves learning to pause before responding, creating space for deeper insight to emerge. Many breakthroughs occur in the pause after a client finish speaking, when they feel fully heard and additional clarity surfaces. Notice your client's metaphors, recurring phrases, and communication patterns. Someone who consistently uses competitive language might benefit from exploring collaborative approaches.

Pay attention to changes in your client's energy and engagement throughout the session. When do they become more animated? When do they seem to withdraw? These indicators often point toward what's most important for optimal performance.

Common obstacles include the solution reflex of immediately moving to recommendations without fully understanding complexity, getting absorbed in story details while missing strategic patterns, hearing your own experiences instead of their unique situation, and feeling compelled to offer wisdom instead of creating space for their insights.

Competency Three: Purposeful Inquiry

Questions serve as the precision instruments of professional coaching they shape awareness, challenge assumptions, and create pathways to new possibilities. Masterful inquiry goes beyond information gathering to catalyze insight, challenge limitations, and drive performance improvement.

Information questions gather facts and context like "What happened?" and "Who are the key stakeholders?" While necessary for understanding the situation, they maintain surface-level engagement. Analysis questions invite deeper examination through queries like "What was the impact of that decision?" and "What patterns do you notice?" They begin to create analytical thinking and pattern recognition.

Strategic questions challenge current thinking with inquiries such as "What assumptions might you be making?" and "What are you not seeing in this situation?" They challenge mental models and reveal new perspectives. Transformation questions catalyze fundamental shifts in approach through questions like "What would you do if failure weren't possible?" and "What leadership qualities are this situation calling forth?" They access higher-level thinking and drive sustainable change.

Effective questions expand possibilities rather than limit options. Instead of asking "Why did that approach fail?" which creates defensiveness, try "What did that approach teach you about what might work better?" The first contract thinking while the second expands learning.

Questions that assume competence build confidence by asking, "What do you already know about handling this type of situation?" rather than "Do you have any ideas about this?" Questions that focus on outcomes open strategic thinking by exploring what success would look like rather than dwelling on current problems. Questions that enhance agency give clients strategic choice by asking what feels most important to address first.

Advanced techniques include reframing questions that shift perspective, such as "How might this obstacle actually be an opportunity?" Future-state questions access wisdom from different perspectives by asking what their most successful self would do. Systems questions help clients consider broader implications, while resource questions expand solution options by exploring unutilized assets and network connections.

Understanding timing is crucial. Early in sessions, use analytical questions to build understanding and rapport. Mid-session, employ strategic questions to deepen insight. Near the end, use transformation questions to catalyze commitment and forward movement.

Competency Four: Professional Container Management

Container management is the ability to create and maintain an optimal environment for breakthrough thinking and performance improvement. It's the skill of establishing clear boundaries, expectations, and processes that allow whatever needs to emerge, uncertainty, frustration, excitement, clarity without attempting to manage or control it.

Psychological safety ensures your client feels safe to think out loud, admit uncertainty, challenge their own assumptions, and explore unconventional approaches. This safety isn't created through reassurance but through your consistent demonstration of professional competence and non-judgmental engagement. Develop standard responses that communicate acceptance, such as "That's a natural concern" and "Many high performers face similar challenges."

Clear boundaries require being fully engaged without taking responsibility for your client's decisions or outcomes. You remain supportively connected while maintaining appropriate professional distance. After each session, practice professional closure by reviewing your notes, identifying key insights, and mentally transitioning out of the client relationship until the next session.

Professional neutrality isn't indifference but rather professional objectivity that allows your client to be exactly where they are without your agenda for where they should be. Your neutrality creates freedom for their authentic assessment and decision-making. Notice when you have preferences for your client's choices and practice maintaining support for their decision-making process while releasing attachment to specific outcomes.

Strategic awareness involves maintaining perspective that can hold both their current challenges and their emerging capabilities. You see both immediate issues and longer-term development opportunities. Develop the ability to track multiple dimensions simultaneously their stated concerns, underlying patterns, emotional dynamics, and strategic possibilities without losing professional focus.

Common challenges include the consultant's dilemma of wanting to provide direction when clients face difficult decisions, but premature advice-giving reduces clients' confidence in their own judgment. The expert's impatience with maintaining exploratory focus when solutions seem obvious, though premature conclusions often address symptoms rather than root causes. The coach's over-involvement can lead to becoming too invested in clients' outcomes, losing the capacity to provide objective perspective.

Advanced skills include managing complexity for high-performing clients who face multi-faceted challenges with no clear right answers, managing uncertainty during periods when breakthrough emerges from not-knowing, and managing timeline expectations while maintaining momentum since performance improvement has its own rhythm.

Competency Five: Performance Activation

While deep insight creates possibility, sustainable change requires systematic implementation. Performance activation is the ability to help clients bridge the gap between recognizing new approaches and consistently executing them in their professional lives. This is where coaching moves from interesting conversation to measurable impact.

Mindset shifts involve changes in how your client approaches situations, shifts in perspective, mental models, or decision-making frameworks. Approaching conflict as an opportunity for stronger solutions is a mindset shift that can transform leadership effectiveness. Behavioral changes are specific, observable actions like having strategic conversations, implementing new processes, or establishing different boundaries. System improvements are commitments to ongoing development processes such as executive education, peer advisory groups, or feedback systems that represent investments in long-term performance enhancement.

The brain resists major disruptions but accepts incremental improvements. Starting with high-impact, low-effort actions like spending five minutes each morning reviewing priorities is more likely to stick than completely reorganizing time management systems. Small changes build neural pathways and create momentum.

New behaviors sustain better when connected to established patterns. Integrating with existing routines, like spending ten minutes documenting lessons learned after weekly team meetings, leverages existing structure. Willpower is limited, but systems are powerful. Helping clients design their professional environment to support desired changes multiplies their implementation success.

Guide clients to clearly envision themselves successfully implementing their desired changes through success visualization, which creates neural pathways that make new behaviors feel familiar and achievable. Rather than assuming positive intention will sustain change, help clients identify likely implementation challenges through obstacle analysis and develop specific strategies for each one.

Different clients respond to different accountability structures. Some benefit from external check-ins, others from internal tracking systems, and still others from peer support. Match the structure to their motivation style. Acknowledging advancement reinforces new behaviors, so help clients design meaningful ways to recognize improvement, creating positive reinforcement cycles that sustain momentum.

Common obstacles include perfectionism paralysis, where clients won't start unless they can implement perfectly, complexity overwhelm from attempting too many changes simultaneously, motivation dependency of waiting to feel motivated before taking action, and binary thinking where one missed day means complete failure. Solutions involve reframing changes as experiments, identifying keystone behaviors, teaching that implementation creates motivation, and building resilience strategies into implementation plans.

The Integration: Professional Excellence

These five competencies don't operate independently they integrate seamlessly to create the conditions for exceptional coaching outcomes. Your executive presence creates the foundation for strategic listening, which reveals the questions that drive insight, which creates the container for breakthrough, which naturally leads to committed implementation.

Mastery isn't about perfecting each competency in isolation; it's about integrating them with such skill that they become invisible to your client while generating profound results. The journey to mastery is ongoing because these skills deepen continuously. Each client, each engagement, each breakthrough teaches you something new about the professional art of coaching.

Your commitment to developing these competencies enhances not only your professional effectiveness but your entire approach to professional relationships. In learning to facilitate others' development, you continuously develop yourself, becoming a living example of what's possible when someone commits fully to professional excellence and service to others' success.

CHAPTER 21
Rebranding Yourself as a Coach

Here's What I've Learned About You

You know what? After all these chapters together, I can tell something about you. You're not just going through the motions anymore. You've had those sessions, the ones where everything just clicked, where your client had that breakthrough moment, where you walked away thinking, "That's why I do this work."

And here's what I bet happened in those sessions: you weren't trying to be anyone else. You weren't following a script or worrying about whether you sounded "coach-like" enough. You were just... you. Fully present, completely authentic, bringing your whole self to that conversation.

That's the profound direction I want you to lean into. Because here's the thing, and this might sting a little being technically good at coaching isn't enough anymore. Sorry, but it's true.

Let's Talk About the Elephant in the Room

The coaching world is absolutely saturated. I mean, completely flooded with people calling themselves coaches. Professional networks online are crawling with them. Social media feeds overflow with their promotional videos and self-proclaimed expertise. Your neighbor probably just got certified last month.

And you know what most of them are doing? They're all trying to sound the same. They're using the same buzzwords, offering the same promises, posting the same motivational quotes. They think that if they just get one more certification or learn one more technique, they'll finally stand out.

But here's what I've discovered after working with hundreds of coaches: your techniques aren't your superpower. You are.

The coaches who are absolutely crushing it, the ones with waiting lists, the ones clients rave about, the ones who are booked solid, they're not necessarily the most technically skilled. They're the ones who have figured out how to show up as themselves and own it completely.

Now, let me ask you something: Are you ready to stop blending in and start standing out? Because that's what rebranding your identity is really about.

CHAPTER 22

What I Mean by Rebranding Your Identity

Hold on before you start thinking I'm talking about getting a new logo or changing your social media handle, let me be clear. This isn't about your external brand (though we'll get to that). This is about consciously choosing who you are when you show up to coach.

You're not changing who you are fundamentally. You're just getting really intentional about which parts of yourself you bring forward. You're stepping into the version of yourself that creates the most powerful transformations.

Think about it this way: you probably show up differently when you're with your best friend versus when you're at a formal business meeting, right? Same person, different expression. That's what we're talking about here is finding your most powerful coaching expression and owning it completely.

Let Me Break This Down for You

Your Transformation Story Matters

Every coach I know who's making a real impact has a story. Not a victim story, not a "look how perfect my life is now" story, but a real, honest transformation story.

What's yours? What happened to you that fundamentally changed how you see the world? What shift did you make that now gives you the ability to help others make similar shifts?

Maybe you went from people-pleasing to setting boundaries. Maybe you transformed your relationship with money. Maybe you learned to trust yourself after years of seeking validation from others.

This isn't about oversharing or making it all about you. It's about understanding that your personal transformation is what gives you credibility and empathy. It's what makes clients think, "This person gets it. They've been where I am."

Your transformation story becomes the foundation of everything else we're going to talk about.

Finding Your Coaching Archetype

Here's something I want you to try: think about your most successful coaching sessions. When you were really in the zone, really making a difference how were you showing up?

Were you the compassionate guide, creating a safe space for your client to explore? Were you the loving challenger, pushing them past their excuses? Were you the visionary catalyst, helping them see possibilities they never imagined?

There's no right or wrong answer here. The point is to recognize your natural pattern. Because when you try to be all things to all people, you end up being nothing special to anyone.

I worked with a coach who kept trying to be this gentle, nurturing type because she thought that's what coaches were supposed to be. But her most powerful sessions happened when she gave clients the direct, no-nonsense feedback they needed to hear. Once she owned her archetype as "the truth-teller," everything changed. Her clients started getting better results, and she started attracting people who specifically wanted someone who would call them on their stuff.

What's your natural way of creating change? Own it.

Your Unique Methodology

Now, I'm not asking you to invent some fancy system and trademark it. But I am asking you to get clear about how you actually help people transform.

Look at your most successful clients. What was the journey you took them on? What was the pattern? Maybe you always start by helping them get crystal clear on their values. Maybe you focus on identifying limiting beliefs first. Maybe you dive straight into action planning.

There's a method to what you do, even if you haven't named it yet. When you can articulate that method clearly, clients know what to expect. They can see the journey ahead, and that creates confidence and trust.

Your Signature Presence

This one's huge. Your presence the energy you bring, the quality of attention you offer is often more important than any technique you use.

Some coaches create change through their calm, grounded presence. Others do it through their infectious enthusiasm. Some through their fierce compassion, others through their gentle humor.

How do you create the container for transformation? What's the feeling your clients get when they're in session with you? That's your signature presence, and it's absolutely unique to you.

Making It All Match

Here's where a lot of coaches mess up: they figure out who they are internally, but then their external brand their website, their marketing, their social media tells a completely different story.

Your external brand needs to match your internal truth. If you're naturally direct and challenging, don't create a soft, ethereal brand because you think that's what people want. If you're warm and nurturing, don't try to sound like a hard-hitting business coach because you think that's more credible.

When everything aligns when who you are matches what you put out into the world you attract people who are genuinely excited to work with you specifically.

How to Actually Do This: The Real Talk

Step 1: Get Brutally Honest with Yourself

I want you to look at your best and worst coaching sessions. Your best ones: what parts of yourself showed up? What energy did you bring? How were you relating to your client?

Your struggling ones: where were you trying to be someone you're not? Where were you second-guessing yourself or using techniques that felt forced?

This isn't about beating yourself up. It's about recognizing the difference between when you're authentic and when you're performing.

Step 2: Ask Your Clients

Reach out to your most successful clients the ones who got amazing results, who loved working with you. Ask them: "How would you describe my coaching style to a friend? What did you find most valuable about our work together?"

Their answers will probably surprise you. They'll point out things about you that you take for granted or don't even realize you're doing.

Step 3: Write Your Identity Statement

Based on what you've discovered, write a statement about who you are as a coach. Not a marketing tagline a personal manifesto. Something like:

"I help ambitious women stop second-guessing themselves by sharing the direct, practical truth they need to hear, wrapped in genuine care and belief in their potential. "Or:

"I guide creative entrepreneurs to trust their intuition and take bold action by creating a safe space for exploration and combining strategic thinking with emotional support."

This statement becomes your North Star. Everything you do should align with it.

Step 4: Test It Out

Start showing up as this version of yourself. In your sessions, in your marketing, in your conversations with potential clients. Pay attention to how it feels and how people respond.

If it feels energizing and authentic, and if you're attracting people who are excited to work with you, you're on the right track. If something feels misaligned, recalibrate.

The Scary Part, But Also the Exciting Part

Here's what nobody tells you about rebranding your identity: it's terrifying. Because it means making choices. It means saying, "This is who I am and who I serve," which automatically means saying, "This is who I'm not and who I don't serve."

You might lose some potential clients. You might have people who don't resonate with your approach. And that's exactly the point.

When you try to appeal to everyone, you inspire no one. When you dare to be specifically yourself, you become magnetic to the right people.

I know a coach who was struggling to fill her programs. She was trying to be everything to everyone mindset coach, business strategist, spiritual guide, and relationship expert. When she narrowed her focus to helping women entrepreneurs overcome imposter syndrome (something she'd struggled with herself), she went from barely making ends meet to having a six-month waiting list.

Same person, same skills, but she finally owned who she was.

What Happens When You Get This Right

When you successfully rebrand your identity as a coach, everything shifts. You start attracting clients who are specifically looking for someone like you, not just any coach. Your sessions become more powerful because you're operating from your zone of genius. Your marketing becomes easier because you're just sharing who you are instead of trying to convince people you're something you're not.

But the best part? Your work becomes deeply fulfilling. You're not just another coach trying to make a living. You're a unique catalyst for transformation, offering something nobody else can offer in quite the same way.

Your Next Move

Remember that realization you had about your most successful sessions how they happened when you showed up as your most authentic self?

That wasn't an accident. That was you glimpsing your true potential as a coach.

Now it's time to stop making that authenticity an accident and start making it your brand.

You've learned the techniques. You've developed the skills. You've had the successful sessions. Now it's time to step fully into who you are as a coach and own it completely.

The world doesn't need another cookie-cutter coach. It needs *you* the real, unfiltered you. The one who stops playing it safe. The one who shows up fully and creates transformation not despite who you are, but *because* of who you are. So, the question is: are you ready to own that?

Here's my challenge to you: stop playing small, stop trying to fit in, and start standing out. Your clients are waiting for the coach only you can be.

Are you ready to show up as that person?

A Personal Letter to You

Dear Fellow Coach,

As I finish writing this book, I can't help but think about you wherever you are on your coaching journey right now.

Maybe you're just starting, wondering if you really have what it takes. Maybe you're already established but feeling stuck. Or maybe you're somewhere in between, having tasted success but still figuring out how to make it all come together consistently.

Wherever you are, I want you to know something: I see you.

I see the late nights learning new techniques, the money invested in certifications, the moments of doubt when you wonder if you're making a real difference. But I also see your heart. I see why you chose this path because something inside you knows you're meant to help people transform their lives.

That knowing? That deep sense of purpose? That's not something you can learn from a book. That's something you were born with. And it's exactly what the world needs right now.

Here's what I've learned: the coaches who make it aren't necessarily the most technically skilled. They're the ones who stop hiding and start showing up as themselves. They embrace their unique perspective, their story, their authentic way of creating change.

You have something inside you that no other coach has. Maybe it's your combination of compassion and directness. Maybe it's your ability to see patterns others miss. Maybe it's simply your willingness to sit with someone in their darkness until they find their light.

Whatever it is, the world needs it. There are people waiting for exactly what you have to offer. They don't need you to be perfect. They need you to be real.

As you continue this journey, remember that your transformation matters. The changes you've made, the challenges you've overcome that's not just your history, it's your credibility. Your way of helping is the right way for someone, so stop trying to coach like everyone else and start coaching like you. Rejection is redirection the clients meant to work with you will feel it immediately, and the ones who aren't were never your people anyway. You're more ready than you think. You don't need one more certification. You need to trust what you already know and start sharing it with the world.

I won't pretend this journey is always easy. There will be days when you question everything. On those days, remember why you started. Remember that first client whose life changed because of your work. Remember the feeling you get when someone has a breakthrough.

That's not an accident. That's your gift at work.

I'm writing this because I believe in you. I believe in your potential to create profound change. I believe your unique combination of skills and perspective is exactly what certain people need to hear.

But more than my belief in you, I hope you believe in yourself.

You are the coach someone is waiting for. You've always been that person. Now it's time to step fully into it.

And if you ever need a reminder of why you're doing this work, or want to share a success story, or just need someone to tell you that you've got this, please reach out to me: sumaiya@eunoiainternational

Because here's the truth: we're all figuring this out as we go. That's the beauty of this work it grows us as much as we help our clients grow.

Thank you for choosing this path. Thank you for your willingness to help others transform their lives. The world is better because you're in it.

I'm rooting for you, always.

With deep respect and belief in your potential,

Sumaiya Sultana

A Look into Actual Transformations

Recall when I spoke before that I've been blessed to work with amazing clients who've seen incredible outcomes as a result of our coaching process together? Well, I'd like to give you a look at just what that actually looks like in action.

What you're going to hear aren't only success stories they're actual descriptions of the struggles, epiphanies, and overhauls that occurred when we rolled up our sleeves and got the work done together. Every individual came to me with a distinct scenario, and every one needed a customized solution.

I've included these case studies because I think they'll provide you with a real-world understanding of how personal & professional coaching really works. You'll notice the particular issues my clients were dealing with from career changes and leadership challenges to work-life balance and regaining their sense of purpose. More importantly, you'll notice the strategies we employed and the results they attained.

As you read these, you may find yourself in some of them. That's the whole idea. Whatever you're facing with imposter syndrome as a new leader, being stuck in your own career, having a hard time making decisions, or just feeling like something has to shift but you can't quite identify what these case studies will demonstrate to you that you are not alone, and better yet, that there is a way out.

The case study is structured in a similar way: the original challenge, the coaching process that we followed, and the concrete results that ensued. You'll see transformation doesn't come immediately, but with proper guidance, commitment, and approach, it certainly does.

I've altered names and some identifying features to keep my clients' identities confidential, but the challenges, the process, and the results? Those are entirely real.

Let's get started.

Case Study

Case Study 1: Shaking Off Decades of Repressed Pain

Mr. D'Souza was introduced to me through one of my long-standing clients a person in whom he had complete trust. This was significant since, prior to our first conversation, he had resigned from his well-known executive position at a Fortune 500 company in Canada. He was beset by deep depression, was medicated, and had consulted with a number of therapists with no change. He had, literally, lost hope.

"I'm calling you only because of who recommended you," he bluntly reminded me on our first call. "I don't expect this to work either."

The symptoms were disabling: persistent insomnia, incessant ruminating, and intrusive thoughts that could occur at any moment during a meeting, family dinner, or in the middle of the night. These thoughts triggered overpowering emotional responses that felt completely beyond his control. His concern had gotten so out of hand that his vital signs were erratically oscillating. His doctor had been straight with him: "Your body is reacting to what is happening in your head. You need to address the cause."

But what made Mr. D'Souza's case particularly challenging was the fact that physically, he just could not have his eyes closed for any form of therapy or meditation. The moment he did, the flood of thoughts mounted, panic set in, and he'd have to quit. All the therapists that he had consulted employed standard relaxation techniques all of which included closed eyes. None of them worked.

Understanding the Root

As we talked, a disturbing scenario emerged. Mr. D'Souza grew up in a conservative family with a dictatorial, authoritative father. When his father passed away during his childhood, the entire responsibility of the family was left on his thin shoulders. He turned into the bread earner, the caretaker, the decision-maker for his brothers and mother before he had even finished his adolescence.

"I never had the opportunity to be young," he whispered. "One day I was a boy, the next day I was the head of the household."

He'd sacrificed his youth, his freedom, his dreams. He'd worked endless hours, emigrated to Canada after marriage, built a successful career, and on the surface, everything was fine. But inside, years of bottled pain, unexpressed grief, and unspoken emotions had been building up like pressure in a sealed container. The lid had exploded.

The insomnia wasn't about sleep. The thinking wasn't about worry. This was his brain's pitiful attempt to make sense of all that he'd never permitted himself to feel.

The Coaching Process: An Alternative Approach

I knew immediately that traditional methods would not be sufficient here. If Mr. D'Souza could not close his eyes without causing panic, we had to start with his eyes open.

Weeks 1- 3: Building the Foundation

Instead of fighting his habit, I worked with it. We started with "active awareness" exercises activities he could do wakeful; all in the here and now.

Grounding Exercises: I had him notice sensory experiences the feel of things around him, the feel of the air on his skin, the feeling of his feet on the floor. This gave his racing mind something concrete to anchor itself.

Externalizing Thoughts: I used a technique that I prefer to call "thought witnessing." Instead of trying to push his thoughts away, he would speak them out loud in the sessions or write them down at one time. This took the thoughts out of his mind and gave them to him as an external object that he could look at rather than as a something telling him what to do internally.

Micro-Rest Periods: Because he could not sleep for extended periods, we instituted a 10-15 minute "conscious rest" period during the day when he sat comfortably, eyes open, concentrating on one object while doing controlled breathing.

Weeks 4-8: Unpacking the Suppressed Pain

Once we'd established basic techniques for managing his symptoms, we began the deeper work. This was about creating a safe space for him to finally express what he'd been carrying for decades.

Narrative Therapy: I asked him to retell his story chronologically, not as a victim, but as a witness to the life he has lived. "What would you say to that little boy who lost his dad?" I asked. The tears began to flow. For the first time in his life, he allowed himself to grieve not only for the loss of his dad, but his childhood lost, his youth taken, all the moments he never got.

Permission to Feel: Mr. D'Souza had lived his entire life being "strong" for all others. I took specific permission from him to be weak, to be angry, to be sad. "This room is yours," I told him. "Here, you do not have to hold it all together."

Physical Release: Since meditation in the traditional sense wasn't an option, we incorporated movement. In particularly emotional breakthroughs, I'd have him walk, pace, or even just perform some simple physical exercises while talking. His body has to release what his mind was filtering.

Weeks 9-16: Restoring Control

With the suppressed emotions coming up and releasing, we started on establishing his sense of control and agency.

Thought Scheduling: Instead of battling intrusive thoughts every time they popped up, we created set "thinking time." He would divide certain times of the day to deliberately work with difficult thoughts. Paradoxically, this reduced the power of their capacity to surprise him at random moments.

Decision-Making Structure: Decades of overthinking had immobilized his capacity to make even straightforward decisions. We built a clear structure: for every decision, he had 48 hours at most to research, then he must make a choice. No more perpetual deliberation.

Sleep Architecture: Under his doctor's guidance, we fully reorganized his nighttime schedule. No screens after 8 PM, wind-down activities, and most importantly if sleep did not come within 30 minutes of going to bed, he would get up and accomplish a pre-planned relaxing exercise rather than remaining in bed anxious. This broke the association between his bed and anxiety.

Progressive Eye-Closure Training: Once his anxiety had decreased significantly, we progressively began working toward closing his eyes. One second, three, five. No pressure, no expectations. Within three months' time, he could keep his eyes closed for extended periods.

Weeks 17-24: Reintegration and Purpose

The final phase was about rebuilding his life with purpose, not obligation.

Values Clarification: For the first time, we clarified what mattered most to him not what he should value, but what did actually bring him fulfilment.

Career Redesign: We discussed what he wished for from his work life thereafter. Did he wish to return to the corporate world? Start anew? The idea was that now, the choice would be his, one made out of volition and not necessity.

Relationship Repair: His inner conflict had pushed his marriage and family relationships to the breaking point. We established communication skills and emotional honesty skills he'd never acquired because he'd always been so busy being "strong."

The Outcome

Six months into our working together, the turnaround was dramatic:

Sleep Restored: Mr. D'Souza was sleeping 6-7 hours a night consistently, without medication (with his doctor's careful monitoring).

Mental Clarity: The intrusions had lessened by some 80%. When they did arise, he possessed the skills to manage them effectively.

Physical Health: His vital signs stabilized. His doctor reduced his medication and was astonished at the difference.

Emotional Freedom: He'd processed decades of pent-up pain and sorrow. He could now access and ventilate his feelings in a healthy way.

Career Decision: He decided to take a strategic consulting job fewer hours, more autonomy, work aligned with his values and not just his ability.

Relationship Rebirth: His wife told him, "I feel like I'm getting to know you for the first time. The real you."

But most importantly, he regained something he thought he'd lost forever: hope.

The Key Insight

Mr. D'Souza's case did something vital to me: it showed me that sometimes the symptoms we're fighting so hard against are actually the messengers we need to hear. His insomnia, his fear, his failure to close his eyes these weren't weaknesses to be overcome. These were warning bells sounding out to him because he'd been denying his own needs for far too long.

The turnaround did not result from prodding him into established therapeutic modalities, but from entering in with him exactly where he was and creating a bespoke way forward. We did not fight his resistance to closing his eyes we worked with it until he could. We didn't suppress his feelings even more we created space for them to finally emerge.

As he explained to us in one of our recent sessions: "I spent my whole life being the person everyone else needed me to be. I'm learning at last to be the person I needed all along."

Case Study 2: From Resistance to Digital Adoption

When Rajesh Kumar first called me, I could tell from the desperation in his voice. As VP of Ops for a rapidly scaling e-commerce company, he was supposed to be celebrating they'd just secured Series B funding. Instead, he was in full-blown meltdown.

"My CEO spoke to me last week," Rajesh continued, massaging his temples during our video conference. He didn't beat around the bush. " He said I'm stifling the company. Me, the guy who's been here since the beginning, who built this entire department from the ground up."

The pain in his voice was evident. Here was someone who'd invested all he had in this firm, and now felt as if he were letting it down.

The problem? Rajesh was unable to keep up with the tidal wave of automation inundating the company. Project management software, data analytics tools, automated workflow programs, CRM integrations it seemed that every week or so there was a new tool he was supposed to know about. And he just. couldn't.

His team had increased from 8 people to 35 over a span of eighteen months. But Rajesh was still doing it all personally himself personally checking in with every single person, tracking projects on Excel charts, needing approval of every single decision. It was killing him, and it was killing the company's momentum.

"I'm putting in 70-hour weeks and still falling behind," he conceded. "My staff is frustrated because they're eager to work on these new systems, but I keep dragging them back to the old ways. I know I'm the issue. I just don't know how to fix it."

The numbers were compelling:

• Projects ran 3 weeks behind schedule on average because everything waited on Rajesh's OK

- His team's participation levels had dropped 30% within six months
- Other departments had started working around, not with, his team

The CEO had addressed the board privately on whether or not to start looking for Rajesh's replacement. Rajesh knew all this. That's why he'd finally called for help even though part of him knew it was most likely too late now.

Understanding the Root

Over our first few meetings, I grew to admire the real Rajesh not just the struggling VP but the person behind the moniker.

He'd come from a middle-class family in Pune, the first of his family to have an engineering degree. He'd climbed the ranks of traditional manufacturing firms where to be successful was to have knowledge of your operations second to none, to be hands-on, to gain respect through hard work and technical prowess. Five years ago, when he'd jumped into e-commerce, it had been a nightmare but he'd managed to figure it out by sheer will and hard work.

Rajesh had built his entire image as the guy who knew it all, who could repair anything, who never said "I don't know." His crew was afraid and admired him because he'd been in the trenches with them, because he understood all the gory details of each process.

And now? These computer programs were going to make all that irrelevant.

"If a computer program can do my job, why am I here?" he queried me one evening, his voice cracking. "I was promoted VP because I was the brightest and worked the hardest. And now they're telling me to sit down, let the tools do it, believe the data. So, what am I doing here? What am I worth?"

But there was something deeper he was holding back. At one very honest moment, he at last exclaimed it:

"I am dumb, okay? Everyone else just seems to have a handle on these tools. They click around like they are no big deal. But me? I sit there staring at these dashboards and I don't even know what half the numbers are. Do you have any idea how humiliating that is? I am a VP. I am supposed to know this."

His voice subsided. "I watch these 25-year-old kids on my team work these systems like second nature, and I feel like a dinosaur. Like I missed out on some necessary evolution that everyone else endured. And I'm afraid to ask questions because then they will know I'm not here any longer."

That's when it clicked. Rajesh's resistance had nothing to do with the technology. It had to do with fear of being found incompetent, fear of losing who he was, fear of becoming obsolete.

The Coaching Process: Rebuilding from the Foundation

Weeks 1-4: Reframing Identity

We needed to begin with the most difficult piece assisting Rajesh in viewing himself differently.

On one of our initial meetings, I asked him to do something uncomfortable for him: "Tell me a time when you felt most valuable to the organization. Not busy valuable."

He sat silent for a long while. "Last year, we had a massive supplier crisis. It was all falling apart. I hopped on calls with the team, we mapped out the entire supply chain, located back-up strategies, renegotiated contracts. We turned it around in 72 hours. It could have killed our holiday season, but we turned it around."

"Okay," I said. "Tell me what you actually did."

As he talked, I scribbled it down: Strategic thinking. Decision-making in the crunch. Cross-functional coordination. Negotiation. Decision-making with incomplete information. Motivating a crisis-struck team.

"Now," I said, pushing the list at him. "Which of those took personally tracking every shipment on an Excel spreadsheet?"

He glanced at the list. "None of them."

"Right. Your value wasn't in the tracking by hand. It was in the thinking, the leadership, the knowledge of what was valuable. That doesn't change, Rajesh. You just fear because the shape that value will take must shift."

We spent the next few weeks determining this fundamental reframe. His role in 35+ individuals can't be identical with his role in 8 individuals. That wasn't failure, that was learning. A good leader of 8 individuals is roll-up-your-sleeves. A good leader of 35+ individuals builds systems and enables others.

I also pushed him to admit to his fear of looking stupid. "Rajesh, if one of your coworkers approached you and said, 'Hey, I'm having issues with this new analytics package, can you walk me through it?' would you think less of that person?"

"Of course not."

"So why are you judging yourself to a level you would never judge anyone else to?"

He laughed, but it was a tired laugh. "Because I'm supposed to know everything."

"Says who?"

That assertion just hung there. Nobody had so much as told him he couldn't seek assistance. He'd just assumed that seeking assistance would be weakness.

Weeks 5-10: Building Learning Agility

The moment Rajesh started to realize that he did not need to learn everything, we actually could learn. We created what I had called his "Cognitive Liberation" plan:

Priority Stack: I set the top three priority tools with assistance from tech team the project management software, operations dashboard, and CRM system. The others could be secondary. Learning everything at once was overwhelming him.

Learning Style Match: From our conversations, we realized that Rajesh was not a "watch a tutorial video" learner. He learned by doing things, through hands-on activity, breaking and fixing things, having someone next to him answering questions on the spot. So, we built sandbox hands-on environments where he could experiment and play without fear of breaking things.

The Reverse Mentoring Experiment: This was the most that made him shudder. I urged him to request two of his junior team members Priya and Arjun, both native digital natives to teach him the tools.

"They work for me," he complained. "How am I supposed to ask them to teach me how it's done?"

"You're not showing weakness, Rajesh. You're showing trust. You're being, 'I value your knowledge.' That's leadership."

He was nervous, but he did it. And something miraculous happened.

When he approached Priya and said, "Look, I want to learn more about these systems, and I know that you're really good with them. Would you take an hour a week and teach me about them?" she lit up.

"Seriously? You require my help?" She'd felt taken for granted, as though her technical skill was irrelevant to the leadership. All that changed.

The sessions opened his eyes. Priya didn't just show him which buttons to press, she explained why the system was designed that way, what it corrected. She was patient with his dumb questions. And Rajesh learned something: a lesson from her did not make him weak. It made him human.

Better still, the dynamic between the two improved considerably. Priya started offering insights about inefficiencies she'd witnessed. Rajesh started listening. Their partnership became collaborative instead of hierarchical.

Compound Growth Method: We started with one very straightforward use case: monitoring one type of project new vendor onboarding in Asana. That's it. Rajesh became good at automating this one workflow until it was second nature. Two weeks on, he was doing it on autopilot without realizing it. The confidence boost was tangible. Then we added a second use case and a third.

Morning Learning Ritual: Daily, 7:00-7:20 AM, prior to emails and meetings commencing, Rajesh would crack open one tool and simply tinker. No stress of having to learn anything. Just 20 minutes of wondering. "Huh, I wonder what this button does." Some days he'd pick up something he could use. Some days not. But week after week, familiarity grew. The tools no longer felt alien.

Within two months, something shifted. Rajesh messaged me one evening: "Spent 30 minutes today building an automated workflow in Asana that will save my team 5 hours a week. I actually enjoyed figuring it out. When did that happen?"

Weeks 11-18: From Manual to Strategic

As Rajesh became more comfortable, we began to engage in the more challenging work of letting go.

We did an exercise I call "Task Autopsy." We kept a record of all the activities Rajesh used to do in an average week. Then we asked three questions for each task:

1. Do I really need my own knowledge and experience for this?

2. Can the system or someone else do this?

3. If I stop doing this, what's the worst that might happen?

Rajesh was shocked to see the results. Nearly 60% of his time was being spent on activities that didn't really need to be done by him. Approving routine expenditures. Going through project progress reports that were already in the system. Responding to questions that his team could answer for themselves.

"But if I'm not doing all this," he asked, "what am I supposed to be doing?"

"The things only you can do," I said to him. "Strategy. Mentoring. Problem-solving. Innovation. When was the last time you've taken a minute to think about where the department should be in two years?"

He glared at me like a moron. "I don't have time for that."

"Sure. Because you're too busy doing work that doesn't need you."

We started to rethink his role:

Structure of Delegation: Rajesh put decision-making authority in place, and his team knew exactly what they could authorize independently (routine processes below $5K) and what had to be escalated (new suppliers, process changes, above $5K). It freed everyone with transparency.

Data Over Gut: This was challenging. Rajesh used to always go with his gut. "I can feel when something's amiss with a project," he'd say. But now we convinced him to marry his instincts with data. The Tableau dashboard could show him trends he never saw seasonal trends, bottleneck detection, capacity planning. His gut + data were both better than either one alone.

He called me one afternoon, revved up: "I just separated a supply chain issue three weeks before it would have been a crisis. The dashboard picked up a trend I would have missed. This stuff really works."

• Automated Approvals: The hardest part. We set up workflows under which routine decisions could be forced through without Rajesh actually signing off on them. He set the rules the criteria, the levels of budget, the levels of quality and then allowed the system and his people to implement them.

In the first week, he kept looking at the system nonstop. "What if they get it wrong?"

"They may," I replied. "And they'll learn from it. Just as you did when you were their age. The question is: what's costing you more, the occasional small error, or your whole department operating at 50% speed?"

In a month, he'd quit checking. Projects that once took 3 weeks to get approved were flowing through in 3 days.

Weeks 19-24: Leading Digital Transformation

The final step was really about Rajesh owning this change being the leader the organization needed.

He did something brave: he wrote an email to his entire department outlining his journey.

"When we implemented these new systems, I resisted them. I want to be honest about that. I was terrified that I couldn't master them. I was terrified of losing control. I was terrified of being made obsolete. But in the last few months, I've learned something valuable: these tools do not replace us. They free us to do better work."

The response was huge. Three of his colleagues privately thanked him for being candid and shared their own difficulty in coping with the tools. The candidness did not weaken him it made him more powerful.

Rajesh started seeing possibilities he had never seen before:

He identified an integration of software with Salesforce that would automatically monitor customer orders. The technology team coded it up, which released 15 hours of manual work each week.

He proposed a fresh dashboard view combining operations and customer service metrics, giving the company insight it didn't have before.

He started running cross-functional process optimization workshops, something he never had a spare moment for when he was in the weeds.

His CEO noticed. At a leadership meeting, he publicly acknowledged Rajesh's transformation: "Six months ago, I was wondering if Rajesh would scale with us. Today, he's one of our strongest examples of leadership development. He's not only using the tools he's helping us use them more effectively."

The Outcome

Six months on, the change was unmistakable:

For Rajesh Personally:

- He was working 45-hour weeks rather than 70, and accomplishing more
- His own confidence had returned he no longer dreads new technology and tools
- He'd overcome his fear of being a charlatan and reclaimed his sense of self as a leader
- His relationship with his team changed from manager-subordinate to mentor-partner
- He'd reclaimed his love for his work the strategy, the problem-solving, the impact

For His Department:

- Project duration decreased by 40%
- Team member engagement scores regained and bested previous highs
- His team transitioned from being a bottleneck to a model team for others to emulate
- Innovation pitches by his team increased 300% they finally had the time to think, not just do

For the Organization:

- Fit operations now were able to keep up with the growth trajectory of the company
- Cross-functional collaboration was significantly enhanced
- The CEO no longer fretted about replacing Rajesh and instead requested him to mentor other leaders

The Key Insight

Rajesh's tale is not an isolated one. I've witnessed it dozens of times competent, committed executives who achieved success using one skill set finding themselves confronted with a different world demanding different ones. The instinctive reaction is resistance and fear.

But here's what I learned from Rajesh: the issue is never actually about the technology. It's about identity, about fear, about the willingness to say "I don't know" in a society that demands leaders to know everything.

The break came when Rajesh finally collapsed and started seeking help instead of pretending he didn't need it. When he finally stopped trying to prove himself by working himself into a frazzle micromanaging and instead started proving himself by leading strategically. When he finally realized that automation was not stealing his value, it was duplicating it.

And as he said in one of our last meetings, with a smile I hadn't seen in months: "I spent my whole career trying to be indispensable by doing everything. Now I'm indispensable because I've created a system where my team can do anything. That's real leadership. Took me long enough to figure it out."

Sometimes the hardest part of growth isn't learning new skills. It's unlearning the belief that asking for help makes you weak.

Case Study 3: A Transformative Yet Challenging Coaching Experience

A 28-year-old woman from Hyderabad was referred to me by her treating doctor, who believed that a neuroscience and therapeutic coaching approach would support her ongoing medical treatment. The client had been struggling with intense panic attacks for several years episodes marked by screaming, breathlessness, and sudden emotional outbursts that often occurred in public settings. Traditional therapy and medication had provided temporary relief, but her emotional regulation continued to fluctuate, leaving her feeling helpless and fearful of her own reactions.

During our initial conversations, it became evident that her symptoms were deeply rooted in suppressed trauma from childhood and emotionally distressing family dynamics. The client had learned to suppress her emotional pain as a survival mechanism, and over time, this suppression created a chronic overactivation of her amygdala, the brain's emotional alarm center. Her nervous system remained in a persistent fight-or-flight state, perceiving threat even in safe situations. The goal of the coaching engagement, therefore, was to create a neuroscience-informed pathway to emotional safety, awareness, and self-regulation helping her rewire the brain's response patterns through conscious and subconscious integration.

Establishing Safety and Regulation

In the early sessions, the focus was solely on creating psychological safety and bodily regulation, without delving into past events. Since she travelled from Hyderabad to attend the sessions in person, this environment of trust and presence was intentionally cultivated. Using neuroscience-based tools, we practiced breath anchoring, rhythmic grounding, and co-regulation techniques that allowed her to sense safety within her own body. These techniques targeted the vagus nerve and parasympathetic activation, calming her threat response system.

Once her nervous system began showing signs of stability reduced restlessness, improved focus, and a stronger sense of control we prepared to explore the deeper layers of her stored emotional memories.

Accessing the Subconscious: Hypnotherapy and Timeline Technique

When the client was ready, I introduced hypnotherapy and the Timeline Technique to access subconscious material safely. Under a relaxed hypnotic state, she was guided to revisit early memories that carried emotional imprints of fear, helplessness, and rejection. In this process, she did not re-live the pain but rather observed it from a detached, compassionate state, allowing reprocessing to occur without re-traumatization.

Through the Timeline process, she identified specific turning points in her childhood where her brain had formed protective yet limiting beliefs such as "I must stay quiet to be safe" or "expressing emotion causes chaos." As she reinterpreted these moments, the emotional charge began to release, creating new neural pathways for safety and acceptance. Each session concluded with reflective dialogue linking her experiences to brain behavior helping her understand how her emotions, body sensations, and thoughts were interconnected in real-time.

Healing the Inner Child

Following the timeline work, the next stage involved inner child healing, an integral part of trauma-informed coaching. Here, she was guided to meet her younger self the version of her that had internalized fear, guilt, and confusion. Through imagery, dialogue, and compassionate reparenting techniques, she began to rebuild a relationship with her inner child, offering understanding, validation, and comfort that were absent in her formative years.

This process was deeply transformative. The client reported feeling a sense of emotional release, describing it as "a quiet peace I didn't know I could feel." Her nervous system responses visibly softened she experienced fewer physical panic sensations, and when they did arise, she could self-regulate through learned techniques rather than spiraling into fear. The integration of neuroscience principles helped her see these emotional releases as neural rewiring, rather than weaknesses or relapses.

Moving Forward: Futuristic Coaching and Repatterning

Once the stored trauma was released and emotional safety restored, the coaching process shifted towards futuristic and developmental work. Through neuroscience-based visualization and cognitive reframing, we activated her prefrontal cortex the center for decision-making, planning, and self-regulation.

She created a new identity narrative, one anchored in empowerment rather than fear. Together, we designed small behavioral experiments such as facing minor social situations with mindfulness to reinforce her confidence. These micro-successes triggered dopamine-based motivation, rewarding the brain for progress and strengthening new neural connections.

We also integrated gratitude journaling, self-dialogue practices, and emotional mapping, allowing her to sustain awareness and consciously shift her state during stress.

Outcome and Reflection

After twelve sessions over three months, the transformation was remarkable. The client reported more than a 70% reduction in panic episodes, improved self-awareness, and the ability to consciously manage her emotions. She felt more grounded, expressive, and in control of her internal world. Her doctor noted visible improvements in her emotional stability and supported the continuation of coaching as a maintenance practice.

From a neuroscience perspective, the intervention demonstrated how safety, awareness, and emotional integration can rewire the brain's threat response system. From a human perspective, it was a journey of reclaiming agency and trust in herself, her body, and her emotions.

Key Insight

Healing is not about erasing the past it's about teaching the brain that the present is safe.

When the brain feels safe, it begins to rewire. When the inner child feels seen, healing becomes sustainable.

Assignment: Maya Deshmukh's Case

You've seen how coaching isn't about giving advice it's about understanding the person behind the problem, finding root causes, and guiding change. Now, it's your turn to step into the coach's chair.

Below is a real coaching situation. Read it, think it through, and decide how *you* would approach it.

There are no right answers just perspectives that work better than others.

Maya, 34, is the Marketing Director of a fast-growing fintech company. On paper, she's a success. In reality, she's falling apart.

"I was promoted six months ago something I'd worked toward for years. But now, I'm having panic attacks in the office bathroom."

Surface Problems

- Missing deadlines and redoing approved work
- CEO questioning her performance
- Team losing trust and bypassing her
- Panic attacks, sleeplessness, weight loss, and daily headaches

Maya now micromanages, avoids her team, and overworks until 2 AM yet delivers less. Her confidence has eroded into self-doubt and anxiety.

Background

Once a high performer loved by her team, Maya's promotion changed everything. Her new role demanded vision, people management, and strategic leadership less doing, more leading.

Personally, she's under pressure too: engaged recently, with family expectations to "settle down." Her perfectionism and fear of not being the best drive her to exhaustion.

Trigger

After her rebranding proposal received minor feedback, Maya obsessed over fixing it. She redid everything ignoring other priorities only for her CEO to say, "The original was good. Are you okay?" That moment broke her confidence.

Team Feedback

- "She used to trust us. Now she redoes everything herself."
- "She's online at 3 AM. We've lost our creative energy and speed."

Data Snapshot

- Campaign delivery time: +65%
- Team engagement: -40%
- Collaboration: -30%
- Work hours: 70/week
- Impact: Down, despite more effort

Your Coaching Challenge

What's really going on?
What are the deep causes beneath the surface? What fears or beliefs might be driving this behavior?

What do you need to explore?
What questions would you ask Maya? What's left unsaid?

Where would you begin?
What's most urgent to stabilize her well-being, mindset, or team function?

Your coaching hypothesis: What's truly at the root of her struggle? What needs to change for her to recover and grow?

Your strategy: How would you help her reconnect with confidence, trust her team, and redefine success? What tools or exercises would you use? What does success in six months look like?

Risks: What could go wrong? When might therapy or medical help be necessary?

There's a Maya in every organization maybe even in the mirror. Coaching isn't about fixing; it's about seeing beneath the surface, recognizing how identity, fear, and expectations shape behaviour.

Good coaching means noticing patterns, questioning assumptions, and helping people face what's really holding them back.

Final Word

You've learned tools, models, and techniques but real coaching is about compassion and curiosity.

Everyone faces battles we can't see. Coaching is the art of walking beside someone as they find their way back to clarity and strength.

So, take Maya's story to heart. Reflect, discuss, and learn not just about her, but about yourself.

Thank you for reading. Thank you for caring. Thank you for showing up in the way only you can.

Now go out there and be the difference the world is waiting for.